BEST WALKS
IN THE BEACON MOUNTAINS

D0417907

First published in 2014

© original authors/Carreg Gwalch

© Carreg Gwalch 2014

ISBN: 978-1-84524-221-3

Cover design: Carreg Gwalch

Published by Gwasg Carreg Gwalch,
12 Iard yr Orsaf, Llanrwst, Wales LL26 0EH
tel: 01492 642031
fax: 01492 641502
email: books@carreg-gwalch.com
website: www.carreg-gwalch.com

Carreg Gwalch

Best Walks
in the
Beacon Mountains

including
The Western Beacons
Fforest Fawr range
The Brecon Beacons
The Black Mountains

Editor: Carys Ford

Pen y Fan and Corn Du from Cribyn

Llyn Cwm Llwch

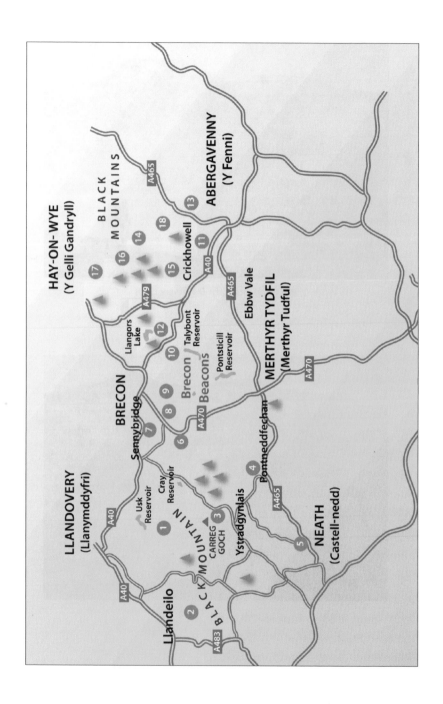

Contents

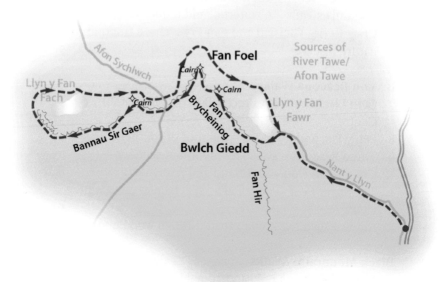

Walk 1

Llyn y Fan – two lakes and a legend

Walk details

Approx distance: *9 Miles/14.5 kilometres*

Approx time: *5 hours*

O.S. Maps: *Landranger Sheets 160 (Brecon Beacons) 1:50,000 Outdoor Leisure Sheet 12 (Brecon Beacons National park – Western Area) 1:25,000*

Start: *Pull-in at, Grid Ref; SN 853 203*

Access: *The walk starts and ends off the minor mountain road connecting Tafarn y Garreg to Trecastell.*

Parking: *Pull-in at, Grid Ref; SN 853 203*

Please note: *No facilities en-route. This area of the National Park is not actively promoted by the Park Authorities due to the ecological sensitivity. Please stick to the route described and redouble your efforts to follow the Country Code.*

Going: *Strenuous – on account of the ascents involved (up to Fan Brycheiniog and Bannau Sir Gaer) and the length of the walk.*

Terrain: *Mostly mountain paths. Indistinct in the section below Bannau Sir Gaer on the return left but follow directions and be guided by sheep tracks.*

The Walk

1. Leave the road, and descend a steep bank to cross the infant Afon Tawe. Scramble up the opposite bank and make for the prominent gash ahead, running down

*View from the lay-by in the direction
you will be walking*

the hillside – this is Nant y Llyn, ascending steeply at first, and then gradually levelling off. As a guide, the stone circle of Cerrig Duon should be nearby on your right, and Nant y Llyn is the last gash that you come to down the hillside, when approaching from the south.

2.   Continue on path with Nant y Llyn on the left. The stream will slowly get smaller and slowly disappear but continue ahead until you reach a lake, Llyn y Fan Fawr. High on your left is the long ridge of Fan Hir, on your right are the heights of Fan Brycheiniog.

Llyn y Fan Fawr is the larger of the two natural mountain lakes hereabouts and is the source of Afon

Fan Brycheiniog

Llyn y Fan Fawr – lovely place to stop for a break

Tawe. It lies at an altitude of 1,950 feet (596 meters), some 300 feet (91 meters) higher than its partner, Llyn y Fan Fach. Moraines, or piles of silt and rubble, left behind by glacial action dam both lakes. There is little aquatic vegetation or marine life in the lake, which lacks essential nutrients, although, on occasions, newts have been found here.

3.   Behind the lake is an obvious route of ascent, up the slope ahead, leading from left to right at an angle of 45 degrees. Follow the path as it takes you up to the col

Shelter and trig point on the summit of Fan Brycheiniog

Views from the summit of Twr y Fan Foel

of Bwlch y Giedd, nestling between Fan Hir and Fan Brycheiniog.

4. At the top of the col turn right and continue to the summit of Fan Brycheiniog, difficult to miss on account of a substantial stone shelter and trig point. From the summit continue northwards to the summit of Twr y Fan Foel, marked on some maps as Tro'r Fan Foel, or just Fan Foel. From here superb prospects open up in all directions. It is a splendid spot to stop for a break, to be preferred to Fan Brycheiniog for the views (unless inclement weather guides you to the shelter).

5. The path now continues south-west along the scarp overlooking Cefn Bryn y Fuwch on the right, and descends fairly steeply to the gap which is the dividing line between Fan Brycheiniog to the east and Bannau Sir Gaer to the west. Cross a stream (or occasionally a dry bed), which is the very start of Afon Twrch, and ascend steeply up the slope ahead to the summit cairn of Bannau Sir Gaer. Approach the edge of the hill, from where there is a stunning view down to Llyn y Fan Fach.

Llyn y Fan Fach

Llyn y Fan Fach can knock spots off its big brother in terms of myths and legends. For it is here that lived the Lady of the Lake, one of the *Tylwyth Teg* (or fairy folk) of Welsh folk legend. There are, inevitably, a number of variations of this tale but in essence the story revolves around a young farm boy who, whilst tending his mother's cattle from nearby Blaen Sawdde Farm, encountered a beautiful lady, seemingly coming from the lake. After a couple of unsuccessful attempts to win her (by firstly the offering of hard oven baked bread then secondly with unbaked bread) he finally succeeded by flourishing an unleavened loaf at her. She agreed to become his bride subject to her father's approval. This would be granted on the condition that the boy could pick her out from her identical sisters. This he did, albeit with a little help from her and the marriage was agreed upon, subject to the strict provision that if he touched her three times with iron she, and her not inconsiderable dowry, would promptly return to beneath the waters. There are no prizes for guessing the outcome, and, after the three contacts had been made, she took her toys and

View of Llyn y Fan Fach

returned from where she came. In the meantime, however, she bore three sons, whom she continued to see after her return to the lake, and passed to the eldest son, Rhiwallon, (named after her husband) special healing skills. It is said that Rhiwallon and his sons were the first of a line of the famous physicians of Myddfai. The line is said to have ended in 1842, with the death of Sir Rice Williams, a descendent of the family.

There is very probably a sound basis for the story. The incoming iron age Celts would almost certainly have been a cause for concern to the indigenous Neolithic locals and their iron swords and other weaponry would have been the source of many a cautionary tale. Interestingly there is an almost identical tale told, centering on the Nantlle Valley in Snowdonia. In addition, most remedies for illness would have had a herbal base and these would have been handed down from generation to generation. Bring the two themes together and you have the recipe for a good fairy tale with its basis in historical fact.

6. Continue westward along the top of the scarp, descending gently as you swing north to the lesser top of Tyle Gwyn. Cross Tyle Gwyn, still following the edge of the lake below, then take a path heading east, downhill, and leading right to the outflow and a small stone hut.

7. Cross the outflow and stay on the stone track to meet a man-made leat leading from the lake. Follow the leat along its left bank to cross it at a small footbridge. Take the path straight ahead, making for the foot of the scarp of Bannau Sir Gaer ahead.

8. Pick up a narrow path that leads between it and the base of the slope. Continue along the base of the hill and, by hopping from sheep track to sheep track, contour around the base of Twr y Fan Foel as it rises up high on your right. Wind your way back to the northern edge of Llyn y Fan Fawr.

9. Follow the shoreline of the lake, either east or west (the western edge under the slopes adds a little more excitement) to the outflow, then retrace your steps across the plateau, down the slope, across Afon Tawe and back to the road and the start.

Originally published in
Circular Walks in the Western Beacons

by Nick Jenkins

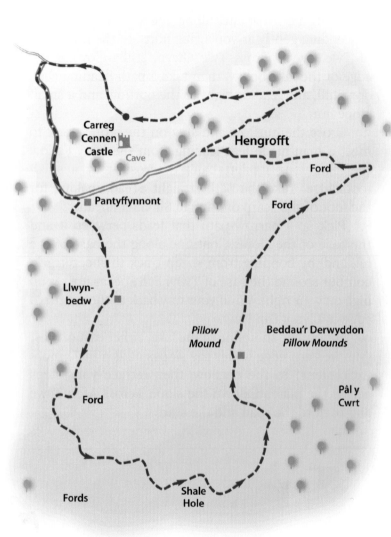

Carreg
Cennen
Castle   Cave

Hengrofft

Ford

Pantyffynnont

Ford

Llwyn-
bedw

Pillow
Mound

Beddau'r Derwyddon
Pillow Mounds

Pâl y
Cwrt

Ford

Fords

Shale
Hole

Walk 2

Carreg Cennen Castle – around Loughor's Eye

Walk details

Approx distance: *4 ½ Miles/7 kilometres*

Approx time:	*3 hours*
O.S. Maps:	*Landranger Sheets 146 (Brecon Beacons) 1:50,000 Outdoor Leisure Sheet 12 (Brecon Beacons National park – Western Area) (Very edge of map, not all of the route is on this map) also Ordnance Survey 186 (Llandeilo and Brechfa Forest) 1:25,000*
Start:	*Carreg Cennen Castle, near the village of Trap, Grid Ref; SN 667 194*
Access:	*The walk starts and ends at the car park below the imposing structure of Carreg Cennen Castle, near the village of Trap.*
Parking:	*Carreg Cennen Castle car park, Grid Ref; 667 194*
Please note:	*Tir y Castell farm has a small but very pleasant tea-room and souvenir shop. Toilets in the car park. Cennen Arms is situated in the village of Trap. Castle is owned by CADW, there is an admission charge for the castle. This is a gem of walk if timed for either fine spring or autumn day.*
Going:	*Moderate – some steep ascents.*
Terrain:	*Mostly grass tracks and paths.*

View of Carreg Cennen Castle

The Walk

1.   Leave the car park by the way you came in, and turn left along the lane. At the next junction turn left, downhill, towards Afon Cennen at the bottom of the valley. After about ½ a mile (800 meters) pass through a gate on the right in the hedge almost immediately before Pant-y-Ffynnon Cottage.

2.   Go straight down across the fields to the river, crossing two more stiles en route. Cross Afon Cennen over a footbridge, and continue ahead, cross over a stile, to the farm of Llwyn-bedw.

Pass through this gate, on the right

3.   Turn right onto the farm track, following it through fields to ford a stream (take care when crossing the river). Continue uphill and go over a stile on the left. Continue through the field, passing over a stone bridge and continue ahead to a stile. Cross the stile bearing to the right

Cross the stile, on the left into a field

The lime kiln that you pass on the walk

The path goes to the left when you see this sign

(uphill) following the way marker.

4. Continue on the track, crossing another stile. Continue straight ahead passing a lime kiln on your left. Follow the path as it gradually climbs going left at a sign (picture). Continue ahead crossing another stile. Turn right towards the mountain road. Cross the stile and turn left into the road.

Deep in the hillside there are reputed to be caves occupied by the sleeping Owain Lawgoch (*lawgoch*: red hand), who will wake and come to Wales' aid when she needs him. This is a very similar legend to the tale of the sleeping King Arthur and his knights under Dinas Rock, just outside Pontneddfechan, in the Neath Valley (and many other places).

5. Follow the road and turn left onto a track, towards the farm called Brondai with many way markers on the gate. Continue along the track past some ancient pillow mounds (I always believed these were for farming rabbits, but

the map marks them as 'Beddau'r Derwyddon', or druid graves, so keep looking over your shoulder). Cross a stile, and then cross a second stile which is on the left onto another track.

6. Follow the path (fenced on either side). Follow the waymarked path as it descends. Cross a stile which avoids the farmyard. Continue along the path, finally crossing a bridge. Turn right following the red castle signs uphill.

Cross over this stile to avoid the farmyard

7. Passing through woodland (the woodland is a Site of Special Scientific Interest (SSSI) and a Nature

The imposing structure of Carreg Cennen castle

Reserve), to emerge at a gate just below the castle at the cliff top. Either turn left and up to the castle or right, down the path leading to Tir y Castell farm and the start.

The castle at Carreg Cennen (in the care of CADW) is a superbly imposing structure, built on a limestone hill with a 300 foot (92 meter) cliff dropping sheer away on the southern side. Access to the castle is by ticket, purchased from the hut passed Tir y Castell Farm.

The castle was originally built in 1197. In 1248 Rhys Fychan captured the castle from its Norman holders but in 1277 they regained it. It was almost entirely rebuilt in 1284 by the Giffard family when they were presented with the castle by Edward 1st. The reconstruction included an outer wall, the base of which can just be made out to the left of the entrance bridgeway. However, as was the way of things in those days, the Giffards fell out of favour and the castle came into the Despenser family. In 1403 the ubiquitous

Owain Glyndŵr attacked the castle, damaging it somewhat during the proceedings. In 1462, however, the Yorkists employed 500 men, at a recorded cost of £28, to finish off what Glyndŵr had started and rendered the castle completely unusable by local bandits (or anyone else who fancied grabbing it). This was borne slightly out of sour grapes as the Lancastrians had holed up here during the Wars of the Roses.

Make a point of visiting the cave in the south-eastern corner of the castle. Access is via a tunnel cut into the cliff face. The use of the cave is unclear; it may have been some form of columbarium for keeping pigeons or possibly even a dungeon.

In any event it predates the castle, the bones of four Stone Age skeletons being found here.

Llygad Llwchwr (*llygad*: eye) is the source of Afon Llwchwr, which flows down to the sea at Casllwchwr (*Loughor*) in Carmarthen Bay. There is a story that an underground river connects Llyn y Fan Fach, under the heights of Bannau Sir Gaer, to the 'eye'.

Originally published in
Circular Walks in the Western Beacons

by Nick Jenkins

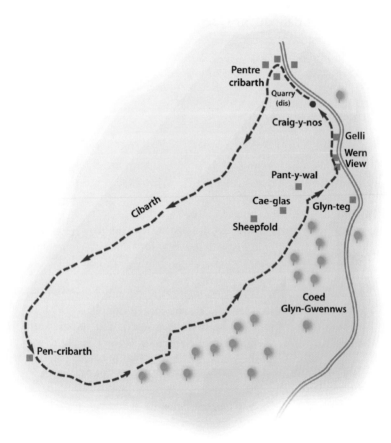

Walk 3
Craig-y-Nos –
Upper reaches of Cwm Tawe

Walk details

Approx distance: *4 miles/6.4 kilometres*

Approx time: *2 hours*

O.S. Maps: *Landranger Sheet 160 (Brecon Beacons) 1:50,000*
Outdoor Leisure Sheet 12 (Brecon Beacons
National Park – Western Area) 1:25,000

Start: *Craig-y-Nos, Grid Ref; SN 841 153*

Access: *The walk starts and ends at Craig y Nos, in the*
upper reaches of Dyffryn Tawe (the Swansea
Valley) on the A4067.

Parking: *Either the National Park car park (Pay and*
Display) or a lay by next to Craig y Nos castle at
SN 841 153 (room for about 8 cars).

Please note: *Path is a little vague on Cribarth ridge and on part*
of the return leg, no serious navigational problems.
Last few hundred yards return along a busy main
road, verges in places to walk on (no right of way
through adjacent fields). Path is muddy in places
and slightly overgrown but is still visible.

Going: *Easy – One exception on the ascent of Cribarth.*
Good footpaths, well waymarked.

Terrain: *Mostly grass tracks and paths.*

Cribarth is well worth the climb if only for the superb
views up the Upper Swansea (or Tawe) Valley, and

Craig y Nos castle

down to Craig y Nos castle. Whilst of modest height (only 1,388 feet/423 meters) it is a ridge that amply repays exploration. It provides an interesting spot for a picnic, excellent facilities for hide and seek and a busy study site for industrial archaeologists. The rock is limestone and was clearly the subject of extensive quarrying around the turn of the last century. A major fault in the limestone runs north-east from here. Whilst of no particular consequences, you may wish to know that I picked up the only fossil (of a sea shell) that I have ever found in the Park on Cribarth's craggy top.

The Walk

1. Leave the layby from the entrance furthest from Craig y Nos castle. Cross the main road and turn left. After about 10 yards/meters turn right through a gap in the wall and cross a double stile or go through the kissing gate which is situated to the left. Carry on uphill for approximately 50 yards (46 meters), following the 'Open Hill' sign. Take a sharp right further up the hill (next to the standing stones)

The standing stones

waymarked 'To the Open Hill'. This path is clearly sign posted with white painted posts.

2.   Follow the path as it winds its way up the north-eastern slope of Cribarth. Follow the path as it continues to ascend alongside the fence, and cross a stile in a dry stone wall. The stile has a plaque bearing the words, 'New route for guide book walks' – very helpful!

There are some superb views of Craig y Nos Castle and the very top of Dyffryn Tawe, dominated by Fan Gyhirych. The main part of Craig y Nos (*craig*: rock; *nos*: night) Castle

Sign post and posts showing the path

was built in 1842, but is far better known as the home of the Spanish opera diva, Adela Juana Maria Patti. She bought the castle in 1878, from a Mr Morgan Morgan, and remained its owner until her death there on 27th September 1919, at the age of 76. In 1819 Madame Adelina Patti (as she was known) built her own theatre at the castle, soon joined by a large conservatory. This was subsequently donated by her to the town of Swansea, where it is now known as the Patti Pavilion. She was buried at Pere Lachaise cemetery in Paris but throughout her life came to love Craig y Nos as her 'real' home. After he death, the castle was used as a hospital but, in 1976, the grounds were opened to the public, under the management of the National Park Authority (or, in those days, Committee).

3. Once over the stile, bear half right and continue to ascend over open ground to the crest of the ridge of Cribarth. From the top, turn right along the ridge to the highest spot, marked by a trig point (grid ref SN 828 143). Pick your own route to the trig point, but there is tram track that almost leads you there. Take care in mist; the quarry workings can loom up on you quite unexpectedly.

The hill may be relatively low at 1,388 feet (423

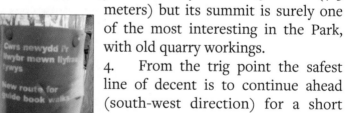

meters) but its summit is surely one of the most interesting in the Park, with old quarry workings.

4. From the trig point the safest line of decent is to continue ahead (south-west direction) for a short distance and make your way to the left down a grassy slope to a well maintained dry stone wall below.

Sign on the style Follow the line of the wall to where

Craig y Nos Nature Country Park

the slope levels off and the path turns sharp left. Continue ahead along a raised tram track from about 10 yards/metres and then turn left along the path, keeping the wall and fence about 20 yards (18 metres) away on your left. After about 50 yards (46 metres) take the very feint path which descends to a stile in the fence, marked by a very obvious wooden waymark post. Cross the stile and turn right to follow a grass path, which contours the southern slopes of Cribarth.

Look out for what appears to be the remains of an old farmstead.

5. Where the path meets the tramway coming down the hillside (marked by a stumpy knee high waymark post) turn right and descend along the tramway for about 10 yards/metres, then turn left, and continue on around the hillside. Do not cross over the stile (waymarked to Abercrave) at the point where the tramway meets the fence. Follow the path sign posted Ynyswen. Follow this path as it gently descends, over

rather slabby rock in places, to meet a stile leading into a field on the left (passing first an underground reservoir on the right). The approach to the stile can be very boggy (a board walk in one area).

6.   Cross the stile into the field, keeping a stone wall and woodland on your right. Cross the field to leave over a second stile and continue ahead across the next field, still keeping the wall on your right. Cross over a third stile, continue across the field, and leave by a fourth stile, this time back in to open moorland.

Look (and listen) out for jays (known in Welsh as Sgrech y Coed, the screacher of the wood) here.

7.   Continue ahead along a vague path, keeping a fence on your left. Take the left path in the fork ahead. Where the fence turns sharp left up the hillside, cross a broken stone wall (look for a way marker arrow on the corner fencepost), climb gently for about 20 yards (18 metres) then follow the path to the right as it continues to contour the eastern flank of Cribarth (no clear path across the field, but wall is very obvious). Cross a stile in a stone wall, and continue ahead over another vague path. About 500 yards (450 metres) from the stile, trend right to pick up a more obvious path which decsends to a stone wall below on your right. As a guide, the short descent to the wall starts opposite an obvious grassy slope descending from Cribarth's summit ridge, flanked by two prominent limestone crags.

8.   Pass through an iron gate in the wall and continue to descend, through bracken. About 100 yards (92 metres) after the gate, the path swings sharp right, over the remains of a stone wall. About 50 yards (46 metres) later swing sharp left and continue the descent down a more obvious track.

Another view of Craig y Nos

9. At the next junction of paths, clearly marked with way marker posts, take the left turn, marked as a bridleway. Follow the path over a tumbledown stone wall (very boggy in areas) and continue ahead to cross an iron stile. Continue ahead in the direction of the way marker arrow. Turn ½ left to pick up a vague track across a field and exit over a stile beside a gate. The track becomes more pronounced and exits the field over a very overgrown stile and in to a track. Continue along the track, exit the field over another stile and into a tarmac lane.

10. Turn right and follow the land down to the main A4067 road. From here turn left and, keeping to the grass verge, return to the start of the walk at Craig y Nos.

Originally published in
Circular Walks in the Western Beacons

by Nick Jenkins

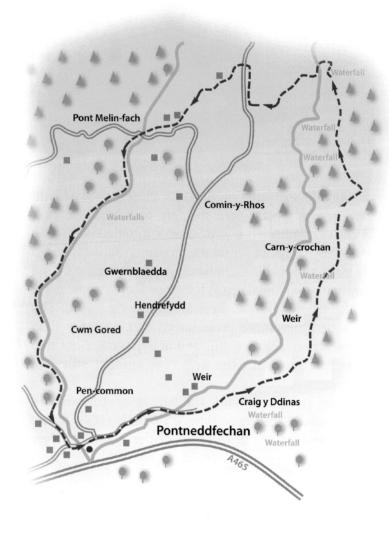

Pont Melin-fach

Waterfall

Waterfall

Waterfall

Comin-y-Rhos

Waterfalls

Carn-y-crochan

Gwernblaedda

Waterfall

Hendrefydd

Weir

Cwm Gored

Weir

Pen-common

Craig y Ddinas

Pontneddfechan

Waterfall

Waterfall

A465

Walk 4
Pontneddfechan – the waterfall circuit

Walk details

Approx distance: *8 Miles/12.9 kilometres*

Approx time: *4 – 5 hours*

O.S. Maps: *Landranger Sheets 160 (Brecon Beacons) 1:50,000*
                 Outdoor Leisure Sheet 12 (Brecon Beacons National park – Western Area) 1:25,000

Start: *Car Park by the Angel Inn, Grid Ref; SN 900 077*

Access: *The walk starts and ends at the Angle Inn, Pontneddfechan.*

Parking: *Lay-by next to the Angle Inn, Grid Ref; SN 900 077*

Please note: *Pub and toilets at the start/end. Tourist information opposite the lay-by with useful information about the area. Small shop with food and drink on the Pontneddfechan to Ystradfellte road (passed en route).*

Going: *Strenuous – on account of the length involved and the roughness of some of the terrain around Afon Nedd. Some steep sections.*

Terrain: *Mostly good tracks and paths, but with some road walking. Expect mud after periods of rain, rendering some stretches slippery. Take care and no problems should arise.*
                 The waterfalls are seen at their best after a good downpour, which is when the paths and rocks around here are at their most slippery.

The Angel Inn, Pontneddfechan

The Walk

1.   With your back to the Angel Inn, turn left along the road and continue ahead to pass the Dinas Inn on your right. Don't turn left up the hill but follow the road ahead, pass a row of houses on your left. Continue

through the village until you come to a sign for Dinas Rock. Cross a stone bridge over the Afon Mellte.

2.   Turn left onto a path on the right bank of the river looking for a footpath sign to Sgwd yr Eira (keep the large and now fenced off, Dinas Rock to your right). At the fork in the path, take the right hand path following the yellow footprint.

3.   Stay with the path for approximately 1 ½ miles (2.4 kilometers). Take a left at the first fork, taking the more grassy looking path (way marker has yellow footprint arrows going both ways). Continue along path until you reach a T-junction. At the T-junction take the left path downhill sign posted for Sgwd yr Eira. Take care on the decent as the path can be very slippery.

These are our first and most impressive falls on Afon Hepste. Sgwd yr Eira, (*Sgwd*: waterfall; *Eira*: snow) is probably the best known waterfall in the area. It has also been known as the Upper Cilhepste Fall, as distinct from the Lower Cilhepste Fall, further downstream. The falls offer a slice of adventure in having a path run behind the curtain of water, attributable to the cutting away of the soft shales by the persistent backsplash from the tumbling water. Indeed this feature was the subject of a fine painting 'Shepherds Passing Behind Cilhepste Fall', to be found in the National Museum of Wales. After rain the falls are stupendous, if a

Look out for these signs on the lead up to Sgwd yr Eira

Sgwd yr Eira in low water ...

... and in greater force

little deafening, a foaming sheet of water crashing some 50 to 60 feet (15 to 18 meters) over a ledge to the deep plunge pool. Enjoy, but do take care; the rocks hereabouts can be very slippery.

4. Continue along the path as it proceeds behind the falling curtain of water along a rocky ledge (quite exciting this bit). On reaching the far bank turn left and follow the obvious path up the steps on your right.

5. On reaching the top of the steps turn left and follow the path to Afon Mellte. The next two falls on our circuit are; Sgwd y Pannwr and Sgwd Isaf Clungwyn. Take the fork which goes to the left downhill, clearly signposted. Sgwd y Pannwr is on the left at the bottom. Sgwd Isaf Clungwyn is a little more upstream, clear path going up to it.

Sgwd y Pannwr (the Fuller's Falls) was named after the 'sudsy' affect obtained after washing fleeces in water with fuller's earth.

6. Retrace your steps back up the hill to regain the path you left earlier. Turn left and follow the path as it winds its way alongside forestry to emerge above the falls of Sgwd Uchaf Clungwyn. Take the path down to

Sgwd y Pannwr

the left to see the waterfall. Retrace your steps back to the top to rejoin the path you earlier left.

7.   Follow the path slightly further uphill then round to the left and downhill to a bridge. Cross the bridge, continue ahead to ascend through the woods and continue along the track, passing Clungwyn Farm, to emerge on the road that joins Pontneddfechan (to the left) with Ystradfellte (to the right).

8.   Turn right, and continue along the road for about 500 yards (460 meters) passing both a shop and petrol station on your left and a chapel on your right. Where the road bends sharp right take a farm track on the left and through a gate. Look out for a National Park sign on the left-hand gatepost. Follow the track, passing Heol Fawr farm, the track goes through a gate into a field. Continue on the path following the way markers. The path descends to a farm, cross over the stile and down a track to the road.

9.   At the lane turn right to descend to Pont Melin

Upper Ddwli Falls

Fach (the remains of a mill being just visible upstream from the bridge on the east bank) and a picnic site. Cross the bridge, turn left through the picnic site to its far end, keeping Afon Nedd (sometimes referred to as Nedd Fechan) on your left. Keep to the path, following the river downstream, taking care in one or two places. Pass first the Upper Ddwli Falls then the Lower Ddwli Falls.

10. The path descends to a wooden bridge, on the left of which are the Horseshoe Falls. Cross the bridge that spans the narrow Nant Llechau, and continue along the path. One or two stretches are prone to deep mud along here, as is the end of this stretch of the path where Afon

Horseshoe Falls

Sgwd Gwladys

Nedd and Afon Pyrddin meet (not so much mud as a vertical bog at times).

In Spring the puddles gather in the limestone pavement between the Horseshoe, and Lower Ddwli Falls are a mecca for spawning toads.

11. At the confluence of the rivers continue around to the right towards the bridge ignoring the new bridge on the left. You now have a choice; either turn right at the bridge and follow the east bank of the Afon Pyrddin to Sgwd Gwladys or cross the wooden bridge and turn right to view it from the west bank (or do both – it's worth it).

12. From Sgwd Gwladys retrace your steps (and cross the bridge to the west bank if necessary) and continue

along the clear path down the course of the Nedd.
After about a mile (1.6 kilometers) you will emerge
back behind the Angel Inn and the start of the walk.

Originally published in
Circular Walks in the Western Beacons

by Nick Jenkins

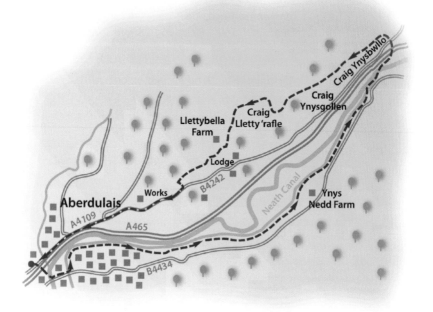

Walk 5
Aberdulais Falls – A waterfall and industrial heritage

Walk details

Approx distance: *6 miles/9.6 kilometres*

Approx time: *3½ hours*

O.S. Maps: *Landranger Sheet 170 (Vale of Glamorgan/Bro Morgannwg) 1:50,000*
Outdoor Leisure Sheet 165 (Swansea/Abertawe) 1:25,000

Start: *Aberdulais Falls, Grid Ref; SS 772 995*

Access: *Walk starts at the car park of Aberdulais Falls.*

Parking: *National Trust car park or lay-by along the A4109. Buses run from Swansea, Neath and other towns to Aberdulais Falls.*

Please note: *Walk takes the towpath besides the Neath Canal to Clyne. The route then climbs through woodlands to a Roman Road and follows it back to the valley. Woods are wet and muddy in areas.*

Going: *Easy – with the exception of a steep hill through the woods.*

The industrial heritage of this beautiful waterfall goes back to 1584 when a copper smelting furnace was established beside Afon Dulais. By the middle of the 18th century, there was a large flour mill on the site and, in the 1790's, the artist Turner visited and painted Aberdulais Falls. The industrial ruins on the site today are the remains of tin-plate works that opened in 1830 and operated for 60 years.

The great waterwheel at the heritage park, Aberdulais

Since acquiring the site in 1981, the National Trust have embarked on a hydro-electric project to harness the waters of Afon Dulais. The huge waterwheel drives an alternator that produces ample electricity for the property. There is also a turbine generating electricity for the National Grid, A fish pass has been installed to enable salmon and sea trout to swim to the upper reaches of Afon Dulais.

The Walk

1. From the lay-by take the road downhill towards Aberdulais Falls. (If starting from the car park you are on the correct side for the path. Path will be on your left). Walk past the falls over a bridge with views of the river to the left. At the traffic lights, cross the road and take the path under the road which runs along the side of the river. Reach a road from where you can see Aberdulais Aqueduct. Go ahead to walk under a bridge

Aberdulais Aqueduct

and emerge on a road. Turn left over a bridge and pass The Railway Tavern.

Just beyond the confluence of Afon Dulais and the river Neath (Afon Nedd), and weir, the Aberdulais Aqueduct spans the river. It is 340 foot long with ten arches. The aqueduct was built in 1823 to link the Tennant Canal with the Aberdulais Basin and the Neath Canal. Opened in 1824, the eight mile Tennant Canal ends at Port Tennant, Swansea. Look for a plaque about Alexander Cordell's novel 'Song of the Earth'. Nearby was the lock keeper's cottage.

2.   After a few meters, turn left at a sign for the Aberdulais Canal Basin. Walk under a bridge then bear right to cross the old skew bridge. Turn right and have Neath Canal on your right. Go around a barrier and walk ahead. Pass bridges and

Aberdulais falls

Locks near Cyd Terrace

locks, do not cross any of the bridges that go over the canal. On your left is the River Neath.

The Neath and Tennant Canals never operated as one company, although they are interconnected at the Aberdulais Basin. At a meeting between Lord Vernon and local people in 1790, it was decided that a canal from Pontneddfechan to Neath would benefit the area. An Act of Parliament was passed a year later. Completed in 1795, it was extended to Giant's Grave near Britton Ferry in 1799. The full length of the canal is 13 miles. Navigation on the canal ceased in 1934. Some of the locks have been restored, and a four mile section from Glyn Neath to Resolven is navigable.

3. After going through a kissing-gate, cross a footbridge over the river Neath. Take a path under the road bridge and turn right along a pavement. After about 109 yards (100 meters), turn left on a path and follow it up the wooded, steep hill. A stream tumbles down on your right. The path soon curves to the left and levels out. Maintain your direction as it gradually starts to climb and become a track. The path is muddy in areas and slightly over grown but you can see the path.

The remains of the old bridge over the river at Aberdulais

4. Cross a stile, to the right of the gate, and at a fork, take the right-hand track. There are soon good views across the valley. Follow the track as it bears right and shortly turns left. On reaching the crossroads, with sings left and right for Byway Cliffordd, turn left through a gate and follow the track, Sarn Helen, downhill.

The Romans met a lot of opposition from the tribe called the Silures when they tried to conquer this part of Wales. It took the Romans from AD49 to AD77 to

Canal docks at Aberdulais

Part of the falls and the old tin works

overpower them. The Romans built legionary and auxiliary forts, marching camps and roads. This military road linked the fort near Brecon with the auxiliary fort of Nidum at Neath. The name Sarn Helen is thought to be derived from the legendary Welsh wife of Magnus Maximus.

5. Go left at a fork and continue downhill. The track curves to the right and has a field on the right. It is very stony as it descends between walls. The track bends left and passes a Sarn Helen sign. The track is wet and muddy in areas.

6. Emerge on road and cross to a pavement, then turn right. You will pass works, keeping the road on the right. Go through the village, passing the cricket grounds and continue walking along the pavement of the A4109 until you reach the start of the walk near Aberdulais Falls.

Originally published in
National Trust Walks (Southern & Central Wales)

by Dorothy Hamilton

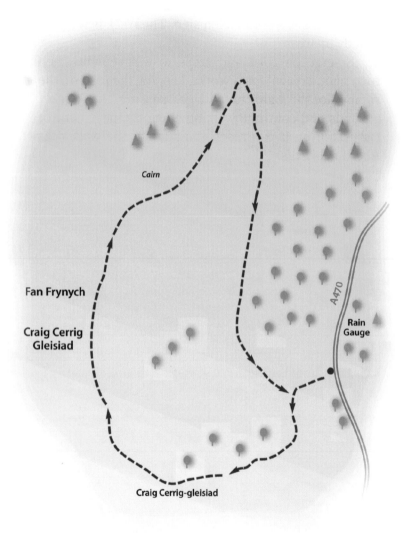

Walk 6

Craig Cerrig Gleisiad and Fan Frynych – a tranquil nature reserve

Walk details

Approx distance: *5 miles/7 kilometres*

Approx time: *2 hours*

O.S. Maps: *Maps; Landranger Sheets 160 (Brecon Beacons) 1:50,000*
Outdoor Leisure Sheet 12 (Brecon Beacons National park – Western Area) 1:25,000

Start: *Lay-by on the west side of the A470, Grid Ref; SN 971 222*

Access: *Lay-by is situated on the west side of the A470.*

Parking: *Large lay-by set off the road.*

Please note: *No toilets near the walk. Picnic site near lay-by. Paths can be boggy in areas.*

Going: *Medium – for fit novice walkers. Steep section to start.*

A short fascinating circuit near the southern limit of glaciations in Britain.

The Walk

1.   In the middle of the lay-by, pass through the gate. Continue straight ahead (passing an information board) up the well defined path. Pass through the gap in the wall. Continue ahead turning left to cross over the stream. Take the path straight ahead and continue

Fan Frynych from Craig Cerrig Gleisiad

along the path as it bears right uphill towards the summit of Craig Cerrig Gleisiad.

2. From here continue to follow the fence and drop down to the fence junction. Cross the stile west of the gate and pass the information board to enter C.C.G and F.F National Nature Reserve. Continue forward and follow the undulating track with the fence to the

Fan Frynych

right. After 500m, where the fence veers right, bear left off the track, follow the path up the grassy bank and proceed the short distance to the second summit, Fan Frynych.

Craig Cerrig Gleisiad and Fan Frynych National Nature Reserve was established in 1958 to safeguard an area of wild natural beauty which is of prime concern to nature conservation. The brooding north facing crags of the reserve, eroded by the movement of ice, provide one of the most southerly environments in Britain for the rare artic-alpine plants left by the receding glaciers. Such plants include cowberry, dovedale moss, green spleenwort and purple saxifrage. Among other plants recorded on the reserve are globe flower, northern bedstraw, parsley, fern and Welsh poppy. Mammals recorded include brown hare, grey squirrel, mole and weasel. The reserve covers an area of 489ha and attracts a good range of bird life including dipper, grey wagtail, meadow pipit, red grouse – one of

Rushes on the Nature Reserve at Craig Cerrig Gleisiad

the few endemic British birds, redstart, wheatear and whinchat. The higher crags and gullies are a breeding place for buzzard, kestrel, raven and ring ouzel.

3.   To return, go back to the track, turn left and follow

at Craig Cerrig Gleisiad

the track down to the fence. Go over a stile next to the gate and follow the track down to the U-turn. Take the first gate on the right labelled 'Llwyn-y-celyn Y.H. and A470'. Continue forward and follow the path down to the wall. Follow the path beside the wall, cross the stream and continue to the path junction. Pass through the wall on left (you passed through this at the beginning of the walk). Follow the descending path back down to the lay-by.

The gate labelled 'Llwyn-y-Celyn and A470'

Originally published in
The Mountain Walker's Guide to Wales

by Colin Adams

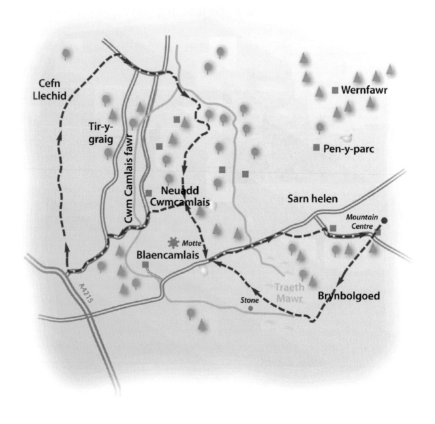

Walk 7

Cefn Llechid – from Brecon Beacon's Mountain Centre

Walk details

Approx distance: *7 ½ Miles/12 Kilometres*

Approx time: *3 – 4 hours*

O.S. Maps: *Landranger Sheets 160 (Brecon Beacons) 1:50,000 Outdoor Leisure Sheet 12 (Brecon Beacons National park – Western Area) 1:25,000*

Start: *The Mountain Centre, Grid Ref; SN 976 263*

Access: *By car: from the A470, at Libanus, follow the signs to the Mountain Centre. By bus: take the service between Brecon and Merthyr Tydfil, disembarking at Libanus. The Mountain Centre is approximately 2 kilometres from here. Throughout the year there are events and activites laid on at the Mountain Centre. It may be possible to get a bus directly to the Mountain Centre on these occasions, check for details.*

Parking: *Mountain Centre has a car park which is Pay and Display.*

Please note: *Toilets, souvenir shop and cafe in the Mountain Centre.*

Going: *Easy – Although a long walk, the going is generally fairly easy on well marked paths. The ascents are reasonably easy, though there is a fairly steep descent from Cefn Llechid.*

The Mountain Centre

The Walk

1. Walk out of the car park, turn left back to the road you came in on. Go straight across the junction and take the track across the common. Carry on across the common with the fence on your left for approximately 1 kilometer.

The Mountain Centre on Mynydd Illtud Common is, the main visitor centre for the National Park and contains an absolute wealth of information about the surrounding area. As well as tea rooms and tidy grounds with wonderful views over the hills of the Central Brecon Beacons, the centre has year round displays, talks, film shows, a shop and even organises local walks.

Mynydd Illtud Common, now home to a nature reserve and Cefn Llechid (to be visited later on this walk), were originally common land as designated by the manorial system of the Normans. Commoners in the area had certain rights of access to the land which

Mynydd Illtud Common

was usually unsuitable for crops. These include grazing, fishing, peat digging and the removal of stone, minerals and soil. The Lord retained all of the hunting and shooting rights. With developments in agricultural methods it became easier to cultivate crops on this type of land leading to the Enclosures Act being passed allowing the Lords to "buy" these rights back from the commoners. All common land is now registered as such and is still essential to some communities for grazing. The two areas of common land in this walk are actually owned by the National Park Authority.

2.   When you reach the gate on your left sign posted for Port Llech, do not go through the gate, and instead bear right across the common. After a few hundred meters fork right and carry on along the clear path to the road with the pond on your left. Backtrack along the common boundary for 500 meters to see the standing stone (Grid Ref; SO 963 255).

The boggy area at the south western end of the

An old pack horse track at Cefn Llechid

common is now a Site of Special Scientific Interest (SSSI). This includes Traeth Mawr and Traeth Bach, the Great Mire and the Little Mire which are important habitats for many bog plants as well as wildfowl and waders. At the very edge of the common is the Felin Camlais pond. Here it is possible to see herons, mallard ducks, teal, snipe, curlews and other waders, as well as swallows and swifts catching insects on their wings. Other birds often seen include raptors such as buzzards, sparrowhawks, the dainty little hobby and if you are particularly lucky, even the red kite.

Near Felin Camlais pond is small standing stone (Grid Ref; SO 963 255). Although it doesn't look much in itself, the stone lines up directly with another stone at the north eastern end of the common and also with the ancient earthworks in Llanilltud. Incredibly, all three line up with the position of the sunrise at the summer solstice and, from Llanilltud, the sunrise at the winter solstice can be seen between the twin summit of Pen y Fan and Corn Du. This takes place at right angles to the alignment of the stones. The stones themselves are almost certainly Bronze Age in origin and as the summits of the mountains were the sites of Bronze Age burial cairns, it is easy to deduce that these people were very aware of the movements of

Trig point at the Cefn Llechid summit

the sun and placed great importance upon them.

The path near the pond also crosses another landmark of historical importance, the Sarn Helen Roman road. This road, which linked forts at Neath with Y Gaer, near Brecon, is more spectacular in other areas of the National Park, in particular north of Ystradfellte. It forms part of a long distance road linking north and south Wales.

3. Cross the road, opposite you is a grass lane, which starts off with a fence on the left and a wall on the right, proceed along this lane. Go through two gates, then shortly before the third (sign post on the right showing where to go) take a track on your left, passing through a gate. This track descends into the valley.

Only minutes after leaving the Roman road you will find yourself walking another historic track, this time an original drovers road. In use until the end of the last century, drove roads were used by the drovers, a kind of cowhand, to move cattle, sheep, pigs and even geese and turkeys hundreds of miles to market. The main routes of the time would have meant incurring large tolls whilst the quiet routes, often crossing open countryside, were much cheaper allowing the animals to graze freely whilst travelling and, consequently, arriving in better condition for sale.

4.   At the bottom of the hill you meet a metalled road. Turn left, go over the bridge at the bottom before ascending again past a farmhouse on your left. After the farm there is small junction on your right. Keep to the left, (avoiding the junction) going behind the farmhouse and continuing for approximately 600 meters to the main A4215.

5.   Here, just before the junction, take a path on your right, through a gate and carry on along this bridleway for nearly 2 kilometers, going through numerous stiles and gates all the way. At the top of the hill a final gate gives you access to the common land beyond.

6.   Once on the common carry on straight ahead, past a pond on your left. At the beginning of the pond a left fork will take you to the trig point on the summit. From here retrace your steps back to the pond, turning left on to the path you started.

Cefn Llechid, at only 400 meters, seems like a small foothill in the distinguished company of the surrounding mountains. It does, however, afford magnificent views over the highest mountains of the National Park and is high enough that it would be considered an important summit in many of Southern England's hilly areas such as Quantock Hills and the Mendips. To the west you will see the vast sweep of the

A winter scene above the pools on Mynydd Illtud Common

Carmarthen Fan in the Mynyddoedd Du or Black Mountains and, to the east, the valleys of the Black Mountains. This truly is one of the great view points of the National Park.

7.   From here, carry on across the common until you meet a gate which signifies the end of the common land. Cross the gate, keep straight ahead and descend in a sunken lane, passing through five gates, to the road below.

8.   Turn right onto the road and follow it past three turning on your right until you come to a farm at the bottom of the hill. Turn right into the farmyard which you then cross to a gate at the far corner.

9.   Go through the gate and follow the track to the right as it drops into the valley. Cross the river Nant Camlais Fach by the wooden footbridge on the left. Head uphill ignoring the obvious track going uphill, head straight towards the fence, looking for a waymarker post (directly opposite where you emerge

from the bridge). Head uphill thorough the woods with the wall on your right and the stream on your left, passing through two gates.

10. You will emerge from the woodland into an open field. Turn right here following the sunken path along the bottom of the field, well signposted. Swing left uphill in another sunken path to a gate.

11. Go through the gate and carry on up the path until you reach another gate. Go through the gate on the right and follow another fence uphill, clearly lined with birch trees. Carry on along the path, through three gates, over a stile and finally two more gates until you come to the junction where earlier in the walk you had turned left. Carry straight on past this lane, through two more gates and back onto the common.

12. Turn left on to the road and carry on for 700 meters until another road joins from the left. At this point turn right off the road and on to the common.

Inside the Mountain Centre

Head for the edge of the wood, turning left along the fence as you reach it.

13. Follow the fence until you come out onto a road, turn right here and follow it to Llanilltud. You can enter the graveyard on the right if you wish. Carry on along this road until it once again, crosses the common, before turning left at the next junction to return to the Mountain Centre.

Before returning to the Mountain Centre you will pass the previously mentioned site of Llanilltud, once a Bronze Age settlement and more recently the site of St Illtud's church. The church, however, was derelict for many years being demolished in 1995. The graveyard itself tells stories of hard times and short life expectancies. It is quite fascinating to think that the church was built on what was probably a site used for Pagan worship thousands of years earlier.

Originally published in
Circular Walkes in the Brecon Beacons National Park

by Tom Hamilton

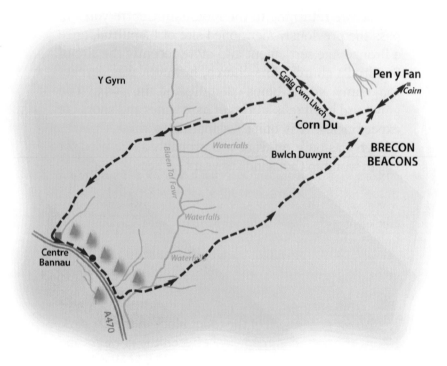

Walk 8
Pen y Fan and Corn Du –
the roof of southern Wales

Walk details

Approx distance: *5 miles/8 kilometres*

Approx time: *3¼ hours*

O.S. Maps: *Landranger Sheets 160 (Brecon Beacons) 1:50,000*
Outdoor Leisure Sheet 12 (Brecon Beacons National park – Western Area) 1:25,000

Start: *Pont ar Daf car park, Grid Ref; SN 987 198*

Access: *Pont ar Daf car park is situated along the A470. Clearly sign posted.*

Parking: *Mountain Centre has a car park which is Pay and Display. Pont ar Daf car park is free.*

Please note: *Toilets in the car park.*

Going: *Strenuous – for experienced walkers.*

The Walk

1. About 50m south of the toilet block in the car park, follow the metalled roadway between the conifers and pass through the wall gate (note the World War II gun emplacement which protected the key pass). Bear right and cross the bridge over the stream, the Blaen Taf Fawr. Take the well established path going to the left (uphill) and progress the 300m to the National Trust plaque (on the left of the path, flat on the ground).

The plaque commemorates the gift of around 4000ha of the Brecon Beacons to the Trust by the

Blaen Taf Fawr

The path up to Bwlch y Duwynt

Eagle Star Insurance Company in 1965.

2. Follow the path up the open mountainside and ascend to the path junction at the windswept pass, Bwlch y Duwynt, where the landscape to the east comes into view. Bear slightly left and follow the path which contours the south-east shoulder of Corn Du.

3. After 600m, at the path junction, continue forward along the rising path and ascend to the first summit, Pen y Fan. From here, go back down to the path

Pen y Fan

junction, keep right and ascend to the second summit, Corn Du.

Pen y Fan (886m) – The highest mountain in Southern Britain, the highest in Britain of the old red sandstone and one of the highest created by sedimentary rocks. The panorama from the summit is extensive, on a clear day it is possible to pick out the Somerset Hills and the Devon coastline. The summit carries the remains of a prehistoric burial cairn which was excavated in the summer of 1991. The excavation unearthed two stone cists (coffins), scraps of Bronze Age pottery, wooden artefacts and a range of prehistoric plant remains in their original green condition.

Pen y Fan Summit

Corn Du (873m) – Carries the remains of a prehistoric burial cairn which was excavated in

Corn Du

Tommy Jones obelisk

the summer of 1978. The excavation unearthed a stone cist (coffin) which appeared to have been robbed, probably in the late nineteenth century, leaving no artefacts or burial remains. Radio-carbon dating of peat at the pre-cairn surface determined a data of about 1800 BC, confirming an early Bronze Age date for the cairn.

4.　　From here, head north-west, locate the steep reinforced path and follow it down the crest of

Llyn Cwm Llwch

the scarp. After 180m, keep right at the fork and keep to the path (note the moraine-dammed lake, Llyn Cwm Llwch). On reaching the Tommy Jones obelisk, leave the scarp path and proceed some 25m to the west of the obelisk. Turn right onto the improving path and continue down slope.

The Tommy Jones obelisk commemorates a five year old boy who died in August 1900. Tommy and his father, William, a miner from Maerdy in the Rhondda Valleys, were visiting the boy's grandparents at their farm, Cwm Llwch, when Tommy lost his way and strayed up the steep ridge towards Corn Ddu. Following a twenty-nine day search by police, troops and the general public, Tommy's body was found near the spot marked by the obelisk. The search parties had understandably concentrated on a wide area around the farm, never considering that a small boy could climb so high. At one point it was suggested that Tommy may have been kidnapped or abducted by a

Y Gurn

childless couple. The boy's disappearance caused nationwide concern and one national newspaper offered a substantial reward to anyone who could solve the mystery. The reward was claimed by a Mr Hamer of Castell Madog near Brecon who found Tommy's body. Mr Hamer's wife had earlier had a dream in which the boy told her where his body could be found. Tommy had died from exhaustion and exposure but how a small boy managed to climb so high is extraordinary. The jurors at the inquest waived their fees and a memorial fund was started with Mr Hamer donating part of his reward. The proceeds paid for the inscribed obelisk which was hauled up the ridge on a horse-drawn sledge. The obelisk is a useful landmark in misty conditions and a reminder of the hazards that can be encountered in the hills.

5.   The path crosses a field of peat hags, gradually swings left and rises slowly to a fence. Turn left and follow the fence past the gate. Cross the stile in the

fence, turn left and follow the path the 100m to the third and final summit, Y Gurn.

Y Gurn (619m) – The highest point, approximately 20m west of the fence, is marked by a cairn.

6. To return, continue south and follow the path beside the fence. After 25m, bear right at the fork and follow the path away from the road past Storey Arms. Once past the Storey Arms centre take the left path at the fork, sign posted for Pont ar Daf. Follow this path back to the car park.

Originally published in
The Mountain Walker's Guide to Wales

by Colin Adams

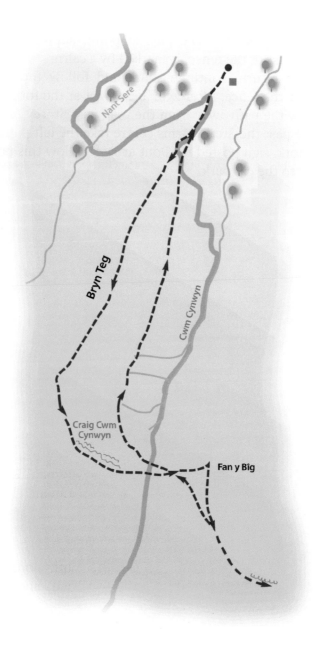

Walk 9
Three Beacons – awesome mountain scenery

Walk details

Approx distance: *7.5 miles/12 kilometres*

Approx time: *4 hours*

O.S. Maps: *Landranger Sheets 160 (Brecon Beacons) 1:50,000 Outdoor Leisure Sheet 12 (Brecon Beacons National park – Western Area) 1:25,000*

Start: *Road-track junction at the entrance to Cwm Cynwyn Farm, Grid Ref; SO 037 237*

Access: *5km out of Brecon*

Parking: *Field at Cwm Cynwyn Farm.*

Please note: *No facilities.*

Going: *Strenuous – for experienced walkers. Well defined paths.*

A classic mountain walk of great interest. Spectacular curtain cliffs. Long impressive ridges. Awe-inspiring pass. Breathtaking valleys. Unique Roman Road. Magnificent scenery. Glorious environment. Long established track.

The Walk

1. From the parking area, head left south along the gently rising track (a possible roman road) and pass through the gate to the National Trust boundary sign. Bear right off the track and follow the grassy path up

Cribyn

the steep towering ridge and ascend to the first summit, Cribyn.

Pass through this gate (National Trust boundary)

Plaque at the National Trust Boundary.

The timeworn track crossing the Brecon Beacons which exploits 'the gap', the only breach in the Beacon's 9km long north facing escarpment, is frequently referred to as a Roman road. Once used by the drovers the track does bear certain hallmarks of Roman engineering but it is doubtful that it is a roman road. It has been suggested that the road linked Y Gaer, the Roman auxiliary fort near Brecon, to areas to the south where other Roman garrisons were established. This seems unlikely given the route from Y Gaer to Coelbren and Neath was by Sarn Helen and the route from Y Gaer to the legionary fortress at Caerleon was via Usk Valley, Abergavenny and Usk. Caerleon was built about AD 75 and Y Gaer about AD 80.

Cribyn – sometimes referred to as 'the Welsh Matterhorn', a tribute more closely linked with Cnicht

The last ascent to the summit of Cribyn

in the Moelwyni. The summit is marked by a cairn.

2. From here, head south-east and follow the path along the curving cliff top at the head of the deep valley, Cwm Cynwyn. Drop down the key pass, Bwlch ar y Fan (also known as 'the Gap'), cross the track and follow the path.

A wintry scene on Cribyn

Cwm Cynwyn

On Fan y Big summit with early morning mist in the valleys

Continue forward along the reinforced path and ascend to the second summit, Fan y Big.

Fan y Big – Characterised by the 'diving board', a much photographed rock platform which projects from the summit over the steep scarp.

Cwm Oergwm

Craig Cwm Oergwm

3. From here, follow the path leading south and progress the 600m to the path junction. Bear left onto the rising path which circles the head of the wild valley, Cwm Oergwm, keep to the path and ascend to the third and final summit, Gwaun Cerrig Llwydion.

A bleak hag-ridden moor known locally as the 'moon country'. The highest point, crossed by the path, is marked by a cairn.

4. To return, go back to the path junction, keep left at the fork and follow the descending path back down to 'the Gap'. Turn right onto the traversing track (the possible Roman road) and follow it across the valley flank back to the parking area.

Originally published in
The Mountain Walker's Guide to Wales

by Colin Adams

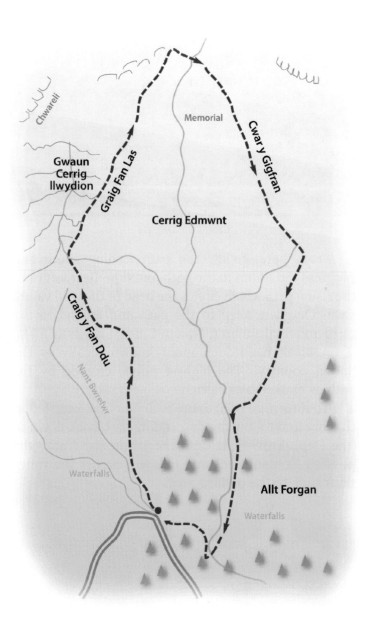

Walk 10
Craig y Fan Ddu – moorland and riverside

Walk details

Approx distance: *5½ miles/9 kilometres*

Approx time: *3 – 4 hours*

O.S. Maps: *Landranger Sheets 160 (Brecon Beacons) 1:50,000 Outdoor Leisure Sheet 12 (Brecon Beacons National park – Western Area) 1:25,000*

Start: *Forest Walk car park on the Talybont on Usk to Pontsticill Road, Grid Ref; SO 056 175*

Access: *This walk is only really accessible by car. It is best reached by turning left off the B4558 in Talybont on Usk and following the minor road through the village of Aber alongside the Talybont reservoir.*

Parking: *Car park sign posted off the road Grid Ref; 056 175*

Please note: *Free parking at the car parks both at the start of the walk and also just down the road at the Pont Blaen y Glyn. Public telephones can be found in Aber, Pontsticill and Talybont on Usk. There is often an ice-cream vendor at the dam of the Talybont reservoir also shops and pubs can be found in Talybont on Usk.*

Going: *Moderate – A mixture of high open moorland and riverside walking, mainly on good paths. One fairly steep climb at the start, two small steep climbs later on.*

The Walk

1. Starting in the car park walk back towards the road until you cross the cattle grid. Take the clear path on your right, leading up the hill alongside the stream. When the path leaves the stream and heads slightly right it begins to steepen. Follow this to the top.

Take this path on the right after crossing the cattle grid

The biggest rewards for walking in the hills are the views and this route proves no exception. From the top of Craig y Fan Ddu the views reach in all directions. To the north west you can see the table top summit of Pen y Fan which at 886m is the highest point in the National Park and, in fact, south Wales. It sits majestically next to its twin peak Corn Ddu (*corn*: horn; *ddu*: black). These two hills themselves are the subjects of other routes in this book.

To the south you will see the summit and ridge of Pant y Creigiau, unusual for its limestone formation in this otherwise mainly sandstone area. Below this the Talybont

View of the waterfall that is on your left at the start of walk

Forest can be seen running the whole length of the Talybont Reservoir. Offering a mixture of broad-leaved native trees as well as larch and spruce it shows off a much more attractive autumn vista than most of the Welsh pine forests.

Craig y Fan Ddu

To the east you hve a vast amphitheatre of Cerrig Edmwnt crowned by the crags of Cwar y Gigfran. You will get a much closer look at these later in the walk. Beyond these the peaty plateaus of Waun Rhydd is an excellent example of the less frequented yet equally stunning upland landscape of the National Park.

2. After catching your breath, follow the path as it trends around to the right and joins the ridge above the

Looking towards Corn Du

A wintry coating on the northern face of Corn Du

east facing escarpment of Craig y Fan Ddu. Your route finding is over for a while as you follow the ridge for nearly 2 kilometres. When the once deep valley on your right flattens out and you meet a path crossing yours at right angles the views now will be directly ahead of you to the north.

The spectacular escarpment on your right drops almost vertically downwards for over 50m in places. These sandstone ridges run almost the full width of the park and are responsible for its form and shape. Often over-hanging the grassy slopes below by over a metre, they offer spectacular photo opportunities for the sure footed walker. This is a glacial landscape shaped by huge ice rivers that have softened the valleys into this characteristic u-shape.

The area is home to many species of birds. The crag itself is an ideal place to see ravens, the largest member of the crow and real aerial acrobats. Great pleasure can be had from watching their aerobatics displays as they soar on rising air currents before

The majestic middle Beacons

diving at high speed, often spinning in flight. Kestrels and buzzards can also be seen fairly regularly, the kestrel hovering almost motionless seeking its quarry with incredible eyesight, whilst the buzzard circles effortlessly above on the up draughts. Closer to the ground you will see skylarks and meadow pipits. The former is always a delight in spring as it leads you away from its nest, usually hidden in the grass somewhere close by. If you don't see one, you will almost certainly hear one as it hovers above you performing a shrill, seemingly endless chorus. Wheatear are also commonplace up here. A little larger than a sparrow, the male is an attractive grey with a strong black stripe over the eye and an orangey yellow breast. Both sexes are easily recognised by a white rump as they fly away, usually short distances to the next safe rock.

At this point the views are to the north. Here you will see the Cathedral and market town of Brecon. Named after the 5th century Welsh prince Brychan (in Welsh, Brycheiniog). Brecon has maintained much of its medieval feel with over 500 protected buildings.

The town now has a population of over 7,500 that swells considerably with its tourists trade in the summer. As well as the National Park itself, the fine Cathedral attracts many visitors as down the canal, where it is possible to hire or stay on a narrowboat.

Much closer to you are the cwms of Oergwm and Cwareli. The mountain streams that wind their way down the valley eventually join forces before flowing into the River Usk at Llanfrynach.

To your left you will see clear views of Pen y Fan, Corn Ddu, Cribyn and even closer Fan y Big.

3.   You will notice that the path to the right splits into two here with one heading up towards the hills and one turning slightly downhill and slightly back on yourself. Take this second path and follow it in the direction of the cliffs you can see in front of you (Cwar

The Canadian War Memorial

y Gigfran). Just over half a kilometre along this path, nestles underneath the crag you will see the Canadian War Memorial.

On July 6th 1942, during a night training flight, Wellington Bomber R 1465 came down in bad weather killing all five Canadian crew members on board. The twisted wreck of their plane lies where it fell and the spot is marked by a memorial cairn, usually draped in poppy wreaths. The Brecon Beacons were frequently used during

The crash site near Cwar y Gigfran

World War II as a training and practise ground and inevitably there were other crashes in the area. This scene however is one of total serenity and few could stop here without being moved. It would be easy to wonder whether the young men who fell here had a chance to savour the beautiful mountains of their own country during their all too short lives.

4.   Directly above the memorial you will see a rocky gully. On its left can be seen a steep, indistinct grassy path leading to the top of the crag. Take this path until it meets a major path coming in from the left. Turn right and walk along the ridge following the path to large cairn. From the cairn follow the path that continues straight on and drops downhill steeply in a grassy groove. This path then meets a wall where you turn right and follow it down to the Caerfanell stream and stile.

5.   Upon reaching the stream turn left over the stile and follow the path past a succession of waterfalls. At the Blaen y Glyn waterfall you will see a footbridge

The remains of the Wellington bomber and the cwm beyond

over the stream, turn right over the footbridge, then turn left after passing through the kissing gate, turn left into the woodlands.

The Blaen y Glyn waterfall is the largest of the many waterfalls along the Caer-fanell River as it plummets down from the hills above. Tumbling 15m to crash on huge slabs of rock, it is truly spectacular sight. In winter it can become frozen solid forming huge icicles, whilst in summer it is not unusual to see sunbathers using it as a cold shower in this popular picnic area.

On quiet days, looks out for dippers in the stream, these shy birds are slightly smaller than a blackbird with a white breast. They can be seen on rocks or even diving right under the water, where they use their wings to swim whilst feeding on aquatic insects and larvae.

As you climb up through the wood after crossing the footbridge there are many other waterfalls on both sides, some supporting fine hanging gardens of ferns and rowan trees as well as many mosses and lichens.

Cross this bridge and head towards the kissing gate. Blaen y Glyn waterfall on the right.

6.   A few metres along this path take a right turn into the woods. This path climbs up through the woods. Follow the path uphill steeply through the trees where it will lead you to the car park you started from.

Originally published in
Circular Walkes in the Brecon Beacons National Park

by Tom Hamilton

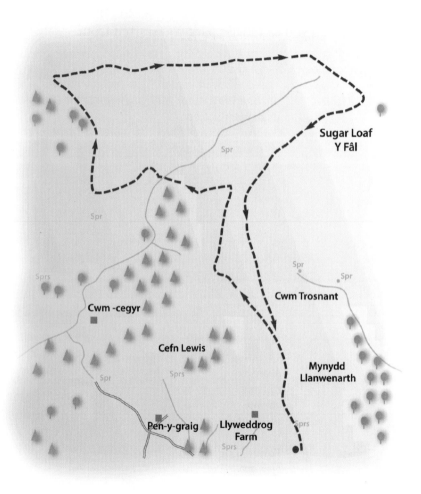

Walk 11

The Sugar Loaf – spectacular panoramic views

Walk details

Approx distance: *5 miles/8 kilometres*

Approx time: *2 – 3 hours*

O.S. Maps: *Landranger Sheet 161 (Abergavenny and the Black Mountains) 1:50,000*
Outdoor Leisure Sheet 13 (Brecon Beacons National park – Eastern Area) 1:25,000

Start: *National Trust Car Park just off the A40, 2 kilometres west of Abergavenny. Grid Ref; SO 268 167*

Access: *By car, follow the A40 west from Abergavenny. Turn right immediately after leaving the built up area.*

Parking: *National Trust Car Park. Grid Ref; SO 268 167*

Please note: *The Car Park is fairly isolated with no facilities. There are pubs, shops and public telephones in Abergavenny. The area is criss-crossed with paths running in all directions and it is not advisable to attempt this walk in poor visibility unless you are skilled at using a map and a compass.*

Going: *Easy – The route follows good, clear paths over open moorland. There are many tracks that could be used to return to the car park, should the weather deteriorate. The climbing is fairly gentle with a short steep push to reach the summit.*

The unique summit form of Sugar Loaf (Pen-y-Fâl)

The Walk

1. From the far end of the car park, take the path which heads slightly uphill in a north-westerly direction. Follow this gentle rise for approximately half a kilometer until you reach the corner of a dry stone wall on your left.

At 354 meters above sea level, the views probably make this the most visited car park in the National Park. The information board outlines the main points of interest, including the summits nearby Blorenge, Mynydd Llangatwg and the more distant Waen Rhyd. Be warned, this is not an area of solitude or wilderness. On a hot summer's afternoon, many people will make the drive to this car park and enjoy the picnic here, walking only a few yards from the car. This is one of the few places you will see

Sign at the beginning of the walk

Towards the summit of Sugar Loaf (Pen-y-Fâl)

the usually hardened mountain sheep happily take tit-bits from your hand.

From here you will notice that there are many paths leading directly to the summit and back. It is possible to take one of these and shorten the days walking by almost 2 miles. These paths, however, fail to offer the walker the real mountain experience and quite stunning views of the Black Mountains that this route offers.

2.   At the wall there is a fork in the path, keep left here and again further on where you will meet another fork. The wall should remain on your left at all times.

3.   The path will start to go downhill and you will see a wood to your left in the valley below. At this stage the path leaves the wall and heads towards the far corner of this wood, now dropping quite steeply.

4.   Just down from the corner of the wood, the path is joined by another from the right. Carry straight on here any descend steeply to a small stream.

5.   Cross the stream. At the fork ignore the path which turns immediately left, down the valley. Instead,

The view from Sugar Loaf (Pen-y-Fâl)

take the path going to the right, climbing up the hill in front of you, and then trending leftwards near the top. After 200 meters you will meet a field boundary on your left.

6.   As the path begins to level out, it curves to the right. Just after this, as it starts to straighten again, take the wide track to your right and start walking uphill.

7.   Carry on to the top of the ridge where another path comes in from the left. Turn right at this junction and follow the ridge. This will take you all the way to the summit of Sugar Loaf (Pen-y-Fâl).

If Pen y Fan is the most climbed mountain in the central Brecon Beacons then the Sugar Loaf (Pen-y-Fâl) must be the most popular in the eastern range. It lies on the Eastern extremities of the National Park and is isolated from the main Black Mountain by the Vale of Grwyne. From the summit, this isolation allows superb views in all directions. The peaks of the central Brecon Beacons can be clearly seen in the distance whilst closer to you the main range of the Black Mountains unfolds. In front of you, you will see the unique Table Mountain tucked neatly in the shadow of the impressive summit ridge of Pen Cerrig Calch. This is the western flank of a horseshoe shaped glacial valley. At the head of the valley is Waun fach (the small moor), which at 811m, is the highest point of the Black Mountains. Unfortunately, due to its almost flat summit, it doesn't look anything like as impressive as its near neighbor Pen y Gadair Fawr which, although 11 meters smaller , has a more conical peak.

To the east you will see Ysgyryd Mountain, in Welsh, Ysgyryd Fawr, this truly is the easternmost hill in the National Park and, whilst not as high as the Sugar Loaf (Pen-y-Fâl), has a much more wild feel.

Often referred to as the Holy Mountain, its slopes are home to the remains of medieval chapel. It is well worth exploring in its own right.

To the south east you can see the town of Abergavenny. Although often referred to as the eastern gateway to the National Park, it actually lies just outside of the boundary. The town is named after the confluence (Aber) of the

Trig point at the summit of the Sugar Loaf (Pen-y-Fâl)

Gavenny stream with the river Usk and makes a great base for exploring the eastern hills. Once fortified by the Normans, it is today a bustling market town boasting many attractions including a fascinating museum. Housed in a rebuilt section of its twelfth century castle, displays of local history, archaeology and industry can all be seen. Also worth a visit is the church, which, amongst others, contains the tombs of members of the infamous de Braose family. William de Braose once held the castle in the town for a short period and was renowned for his cruelty to the local people.

The summit of the Sugar Loaf (Pen-y-Fâl) has to be the best place in the National Park for watching ravens. Although they inhabit most of the area, they always seem to be present here. Watch their superb aerial displays as they rise effortlessly on up draughts before making spectacular plummeting dives. Growing

One of the spectacular views from the summit

to over two feet long with a huge wingspan, on first impressions these birds appear to be no more than large crows. They are, however, true masters of flight and it is easy to while away a brief rest-stop marveling at their antics. If you are lucky enough to get close, you will see quite clearly their huge beaks and hear their strange 'gronk' call. In common with most of the mountains in the National Park, this is a good place to see meadow pipits, wheatears, sky larks and even an occasional buzzard or kestrel.

8. From the summit you will see the criss-cross of paths described earlier in the walk directions. Once you are fully rested, turn right at the trig point and follow the path which heads steeply downhill in a westerly direction. This curves round towards the left (south) as it drops.

9. Ignore one major crossroads then, after 400 meters, fork right at another. Staying on this path, you will be heading in a southeasterly direction until you once again meet a dry stone wall. This is the wall you followed at the start of the walk.

10. Turn left, and this time with the wall on your right, retrace your footsteps for the remaining half a kilometer or so, back to the car park.

Originally published in
Circular Walkes in the Brecon Beacons National Park

by Tom Hamilton

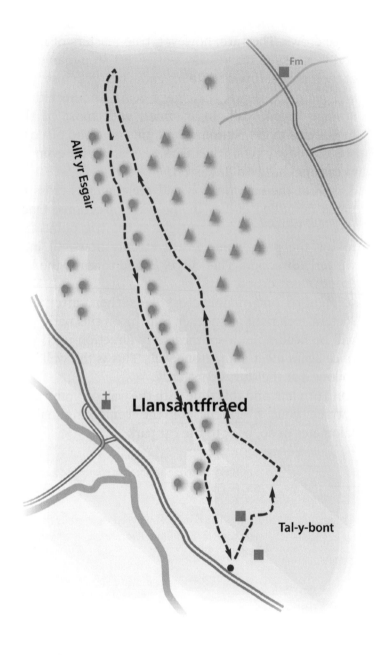

Walk 12

Allt yr Esgair – a Roman road through woodlands

Walk details

Approx distance: *4 miles/6.4 kilometres*

Approx time: *2 – 3 hours*

O.S. Maps: *Landranger Sheet 161 (Abergavenny and the Black Mountains) 1:50,000*
Outdoor Leisure Sheet 13 (Brecon Beacons National Park – Eastern Area) 1:25,000

Start: *Car park/Lay-by on the A40, 2 kilometres north west of Blwch, Grid Ref; SO 129 227*

Access: *By car follow the A40 west from Crickhowell through the village of Bwlch. Approximately 2 kilometres further on there is a large lay-by on the right.*

Parking: *Large lay-by along the A40.*

Please note: *There are toilets and picnic tables in the lay-by at the start and finish of the walk. There is often a snack van in the lay-by during the summer months. Public telephones can be found at Talybont on Usk and Bwlch where a selection of shops and pubs can also be found.*

Going: *Easy – The route follows good clear paths through woodland to the hilltop. The climbing is always very gentle.*

The Walk

1. From the lay-by, walk through a gate and up the

shaded footpath. As the road bears to the left, take the gate straight ahead. Follow the path as it bears to the right and then left. Pass through the gate and turn right at the T-junction. Continue along the path passing through two

Pass through this gate and continue on the path

more gates. After the second gate turn left, pass through the next gate and continue straight ahead, towards a gate in the wall.

2.   Pass through that gate and continue ahead keeping the wall on your right. The wall will disappear, but continue straight ahead. Pass through another gate and continue ahead to the summit of Allt yr Esgair.

Once gained, the ridge after which the area is named (Allt yr Esgair translates to ridge of the hill) gives outstanding views to both the central Brecon Beacons and the Black Mountains. To the west, the peaks of Pen y Fan and Cribyn can be seen whilst to the

Llangorse lake from Allt yr Esgair

Information board at the summit of Allt yr Esgair

east the valleys open out between Pen Tir and Mynydd Llangorse.

A lot closer, the Usk valley can be seen. The river Usk winds lazily past Talybont from its source on the western side of the National Park near Mynydd Du. The river runs almost the complete width of the

Another view from Allt yr Esgair

Llangorse lake

National Park and is home to fine game fish as well as many other creatures including the eye-catching kingfisher and the illusive otter. This shy creature is currently making a comeback in the area but is seldom seen unless you are particularly lucky.

Also in full view now is Llangorse lake, a vitally important wetland habitat which is coming under increasing pressure from recreational use. It is the largest naturally formed lake in south Wales which, like many mountain lakes, is a result of the receeding glaciers at the end of the Ice Age. It is now home to flora and fauna of all types including eels and fish. It also provides winter refuge for many wildfowl. The effects of water sports and farming on the lake are currently monitored by the National Park Authority to ensure the future protection of the wildlife that depends upon it.

On the grassy summit of the ridge lie the remains of ancient earthworks. These, along with the sunken paths give the whole area a very historic feel.

3. Continue straight ahead, descending with the wall on your right. Pass through the gate and continue downhill until you come to a fork in the path. Take the left path signposted for pedestrians. Continue on the path until you reach a T-junction and turn left.

4. Take the highest of the two paths visible (does not gain in height and looks like you are going back on yourself) until you reach a gate. Pass through the gate and continue along the path, passing through two more gates. Take the path to the right at the fork going downhill, sign posted for the A40.

The woodland itself is very varied with ancint trees now surrounded by more recent plantings. In addition

Take the left fork at this sign post

to the splendor of the huge oak and beech trees you will see hazel groves, birch and scots pine. There is now a tree planting project in existence in the National Park. Old dead trees are being replaced by new

Take this path which is signposted for the A40

The summit of Allt yr Esgair

ones which, once planted are generally fenced off to protect them from grazing sheep. The natural regeneration of the woodland has been prevented in the recent past by grazing animals. This has led to these measures being taken in order to preserve this fascinating and important habitat.

Sadly you will also see a number of dead, decaying trees. These are elm trees that fell victim to the dreadful Dutch elm disease.

The woodland supports a wide variety of wildlife. Most commonly seen will be blue tits, great tits, robins, blackbirds and woodpigeon. Keep your eyes open for squirrels as they dive for cover upon your arrival. In autumn the woodland is home to many mushrooms and toadstools. These are a fascinating subject in their own right and add colour and interest to the woodland floor.

At the far end of the woods is a ruined 19th century hunting lodge, the Paragon Tower.

The circular main building boasts a huge central chimney which is shared by four quadrant shaped rooms that surround it.

5.   At the T-junction at the end of the path turn left. Continue along the path until you see a path forking off to the right, sign posted for the A40. Take this path and continue along the path until you come to a gate. Pass through the gate into a field. Continue diagonally

across the field to a gate. Pass through the gate, and turn right downhill towards the lay-by.

Originally published in
Circular Walkes in the Brecon Beacons National Park

by Tom Hamilton

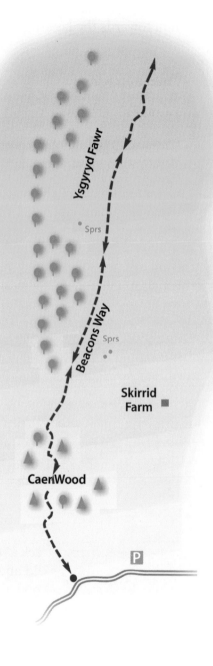

Walk 13
Ysgyryd Fawr – a red sandstone hill

Walk details

Approx distance: *4 Miles/6.5 kilometres*

Approx time: *2 – 3 hours*

O.S. Maps: *Landranger Sheets 161 (Abergavenny & the Black Mountains) 1:50,000*
Outdoor Leisure Sheet 13 (Brecon Beacons National park – Eastern Area) 1:25,000

Start: *Lay-by south of Ysgyryd Fawr (Skirrid Fawr), Grid Ref; SO 327 164*

Access: *The walk starts and ends in the Lay-by south of Ysgyrd Fawr on the B4521, approximately 2 miles east of Abergavenny.*

Parking: *Lay-by south of Ysgyryd Fawr on B4521, Grid Ref; SO 327 164.*

Please note: *No facilities en-route.*

Going: *Moderate – steady climb through woodlands and along a ridge.*

Terrain: *Mostly good tracks and paths. Rocks on the path can be slippery when wet, take care.*

The Walk

1.   From the lay-by, take the stony track at the sign for Ysgyryd Fawr. Ignore a stile into a field and bear right with the track in the direction of a wood. Cross a stile at the edge of the wood and follow the main path for about 30 meters before going right on a path that soon

Seat at the entrance of the woods

The way markers to look out for as you walk through the woods

goes up steps, following the way markers.

2. Walk uphill through the trees and cross over a track to continue climbing, keeping an eye out for way markers. Go through a small gate and turn right beside a wall. After about 40 meters, leave the wall to go left and up more steps. The path becomes stony and then veers slightly right to climb up out of the trees.

3. Take the path up to the ridge of Ysgyrd Fawr. Enjoy the views of Abergavenny and the surrounding countryside. To the west is cone shaped Y Fâl (Sugar Loaf) and south-west is the massive hill Blorens (Blorange).

The ruins of the great hall of Abergavenny's Norman castle where the Christmas Day slaughter of Welsh leaders took place

Abergavenny is an attractive market town which lies at the confluence of Afon Gafenni with Afon Wysg (River Usk). The strategic importance of the site was recognised by the Romans and they had a fort here called Gobannium. The Normans built a castle on the hill above Afon Wysg, and it is remembered for the treachery of William de Braose. In 1175 he invited the local chieftain Seisyllt ap Dyfnwal and chiefs to a

Little Ysgyryd above the town of Abergavenny

banquet on Christmas Day. During the feast, de Braose and his men slaughtered them. A few years later, Hywel ap Iorwerth of Caerleon burnt the castle. Several unsuccessful attempts, were made by the Welsh to kill de Braose, but he finally met his fate when King John took away his land so that he died a beggar. St Mary's Church in Abergavenny is the burial place of several Marcher lords.

Trig point on the summit of Ysgyrd Fawr

4. Follow the ridge to the summit where you will find the remains of St Michael's Chapel and a trig point.

With an elevation of 486 meters, Ysgyrd Fawr is an isolated, red sandstone hill in the

The summit of Ysgyryd Fawr

Black mountains. On the western slopes is an odd looking landslip, and the mountain's strange shape has given rise to a number of legends. According to one story, the mountain was torn in two at the time of Christ's crucifixion.

St Michael's Chapel was a simple, rectangular

Remains of St Michael's Chapel on the summit

A distant view of Ysgyryd Fawr

Ysgyryd Fawr from the ruins of Abergavenny castle

building and its outline is recognisable from the low banks south of the trig point. Only two upright stones remain standing. Little is known of the medieval chapel's history, but it stood at the meeting point of three parishes. It is said that, in the 17th century, when Catholics were being persecuted, more than one hundred worshippers would climb the hill to attend Mass. The mountain was thought to be holy, and local people collected soil from the lower slopes and scattered it in their fields to improve the crops.

5.   Retrace your steps back to the car park.

Originally published in
National Trust Walks (Southern & Central Wales)

by Dorothy Hamilton

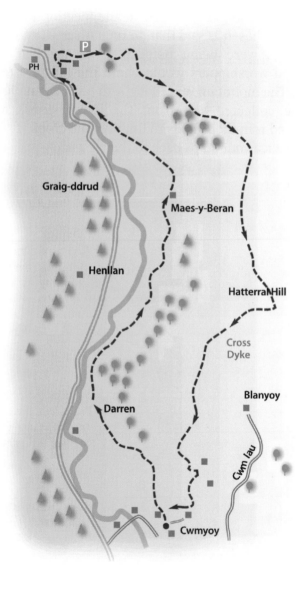

Walk 14
Llanthony (Llanddewi Nant Honddu) Priory – a saintly circuit

Walk details

Approx distance: *9 Miles/14.4 kilometres*

Approx time: *5 – 6 hours*

O.S. Maps: *Landranger Sheets 161 (Abergavenny & the Black Mountains) 1:50,000*
Outdoor Leisure Sheet 13 (Brecon Beacons National park – Eastern Area) 1:25,000

Start: *Car park at Llanthony Priory, Grid Ref; SO 289 278*

Access: *The walk starts and ends at Llanthony Priory, in the Vale of Ewyas (Dyffryn Euas). Take the B4423 north from Llanfihangel Crucorney up the Vale of Ewyas in the direction of Hay-on-Wye (Y Gelli Gandryll).*

Parking: *Large car park at Llanthony Priory. Signposted off the main road. Grid Ref; SO 289 278*

Please note: *Abbey Hotel, situated within the ruins of the Priory, or the Half Moon Hotel, about 100 yards (91 meters) further up the valley, towards Capel-y-Ffin offer food. Public Toilets in the Priory car park.*

Going: *Strenuous*

Terrain: *Good paths and tracks. Some paths a little indistinct across fields on the home strech, but keep an eye open for stiles on the opposite sides. The lower reaches of Hatterall Hill are rather steep, just before Cwm-iou Church. After rain the beginning and return leg along the valley bottom can be muddy, especially near the farms.*

Llanthony Priory

The Walk

1.   Leave the Priory car park by its entrance, and follow the lane back to the point where it turns left, downhill, to return to the road. The Priory is on your right and the church of St David on your left. Leave the

Pass through this gate to start the walk

lane here by continuing ahead through a way marked gate into a field. Turn right along a track and pass through the gate into a second field. Turn sharp right and follow the sign for 'Offa's South', alongside the Priory wall.

The site is exceptionally beautiful and it is only when you force your mind to erase the presence of the nearby road, do you truly get a feeling for just how remote the site is. Little wonder it

The magnificent priory ruins

was chosen by both Saint David (*Dewi Sant*) and Willam de Lacy as a place for peaceful contemplation. I can't think of a few better places to end a walk than here, with the hills above you and a pint in your hand. The poet Walter Savage Landor thought so too, as he bought the Priory in 1809 with the intention of becoming the local squire. For a short while he lived in what it now the Abbey Hotel, but his short temper and unpleasant outburst made him a number of enemies hereabouts. He left in 1813, financially worse off after some unsuccessful litigations, his only visible legacy

The view from Llanthony Priory

The Vale of Ewyas

being the trees he planted around the priory, including some magnificent Spanish chestnuts.

Don't ignore the nearby church, dedicated to St. David, and believed to be on the site of the originally cell of St. David. The alignment of the church is such that the altar points to the rising sun on the morning of March 1st, St. David's Day.

Pass through this gate to start the walk.

2. Cross the stile at the end of the field and go diagonally uphill, to the top right hand corner, to a gate. Pass through the gate onto a broad track which leads gently uphill through woodland. Leave the wood through a gate on your left, and just before a gate, to enter a field. Follow the edge of the field uphill, ignoring the stile on the left (approximately half way up the field).

3. At the top of the field pass through a gate and turn right onto a clear path. Follow the path, keeping a rather tumble-down wall on our right. After about 500

yards (455 meters) the path swings left and starts to steadily climb the ridge ahead. Continue up the path until you arrive at the top of the ridge and a junction of paths.

4.   Turn right, onto the Offa's Dyke Path. Follow the wide track southwards as it gently climbs to the summit of Hatterall Hill. There are superb views from up here, both east over Herefordshire and west across the ridges of the Black Mountains. About a mile (1.6 kilometers) after joining the ridge, look for a signpost indicating a path off to Cwm-iou (small stone sign – shin height).

5.   The path is narrower than the Offa's Dyke Path and leads off westwards through heather in the direction of Cwm-iou and the Vale of Ewyas. Follow the path for about ¾ of a mile (1.2 kilometers) past a small stone grouse-butt on the right. About 400 yards past the shelter the path splits. Take the left fork and follow the path down the hillside. Be aware that it gets quite steep in its lower reaches.

6.   On reaching the field the path becomes indistinct. Look out for a vague path going through the ferns on your right leading down to a wall. On arriving at a wall turn left along a path for a short distance and then swing right onto a stony track (ignore a path over a stile on your left). Follow the track, which turns into

The stone grouse-butt

Information board about Hatterrall Hill opposite the gate

more of a stony lane, a little rough in places, past a rather isolated cottage and garden on your right.

7. About 300 yards (273 meters) beyond the cottage pass a rocky outcrop on the right, known as Y Graig. Immediately past Y Graig, turn left through a gate and descend down a narrow path (information board directly opposite the gate).

Church of Cwm-iou

8. The path emerges at a tarmac lane just outside the church of Cwm-iou. The church is well worth exploring if you feel so inclined – it is certainly inclined if your not! With your back to the church

The valley of Cwm-iou

where you emerged into the lane, retrace your steps up the path and through the gate.

The little church of Cwm-iou, dedicated to Saint Martin of Tours, is fascinating for the determination it seems to shore for not sliding down the hillside. It is built on one of the south west faces of Hatterall Hill which is cleft with a large landslip, similar in fact, to the slip at Ysgyryd Fawr. The church, being constructed on the lower slopes of the debris from the landslip, has becomes contorted as the debris has slowly disintegrated and settled. This contortion is seen to amazing effect from inside the church, looking up the aisle towards the altar and east window. Little wonder that two buttresses have been built on the outside of the structure to support it. I'm told that, of the peal of six bells, only two can rung because of the alignment of the tower! The age of the church is not known for sure, but that it dates back to at least the Middle Ages is certain. Look out, too, for the stone cross inside the church, opposite the porch. This is considered to be of some antiquity, a view shared by the individual(s) who stole it in 1967. It was located in an antique dealer's shop in London, from where it was brought home. Note the concrete base into which it is now set! Also of interest are the beautiful memorial stones fastened securely to the wall. A number of these were the creation of the Brute brothers (look out for their initials); the local stonemasons who were particularly adept at monumental masonry, and are particularly ornate – I love the expression on some of the cherub's faces!

9. Turn left along a path and climb gently between two fences. Pass through the gate, and at the way marker continue straight ahead. Cross a stream and enter a field through a gate. Continue ahead across the field. Just before a white cottage turn left onto a grassy track. Follow the track to a farm gate. Turn right and take the path that looks overgrown with ferns towards a gate. Pass through the gate and continue along the path which will pass through the farmyard.

10. At the entrance for Darren Uchaf Farm bear right following the wall and waymarker. Take the stile on the left and cross a narrow field to another stile. Cross the field and make for a stile, about 59 yards (45 meters) up

Follow the sign for Llanthony through the farmyard

from the bottom far left corner. Cross the stile and turn left downhill to follow a track as it curves to the right into a copse. At the fork take the right hand path, going straight ahead and follow it down to a stile. Cross the field, keeping to the base of a rough grassy slope on your right (ignoring the footbridge crossing Afon Honddu on your left).

11. Make for a stile ahead, and from there on cross 10 fields, passing a ruined farmstead on your way, to emerge at Maesybryn Farm. Be aware that the farmyard here can be very muddy.

12. Keeping the farmhouse on your right pass through the yard

The bar at the hotel in Llanthony Priory

and leave by a gate into a field. Continue straight ahead and leave the field by a stile and make for the field ahead. Keeping in the same direction cross five more fields, keeping your eagle eye open for yellow way marked stiles in the hedges opposite. Finally the path emerges on the road that runs up the Vale of Ewyas. Cross a stile into the road and turn right. Follow the road for about 100 yards (91 meters) before turning right up the lane that leads back to the Priory and the car park.

Originally published in
Circular Walks in the Black Mountains

by Nick Jenkins

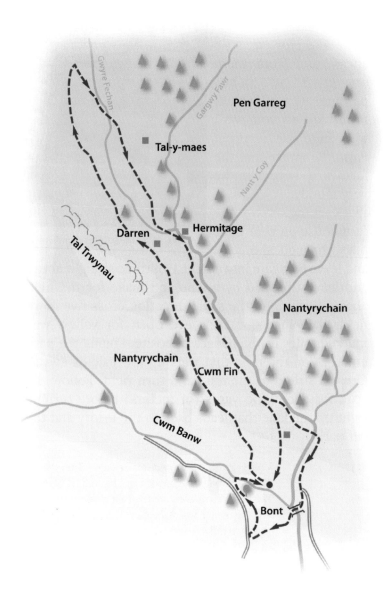

Walk 15

Grwyne Fechan – a remote wooded valley walk

Walk details

Approx distance: *4 Miles/6.4 kilometres*

Approx time: *4 hours*

O.S. Maps: *Landranger Sheets 161 (Abergavenny & the Black Mountains) 1:50,000*
Outdoor Leisure Sheet 13 (Brecon Beacons National park – Eastern Area) 1:25,000

Start: *Near the bridge, Grid Ref; SO 234 228*

Access: *Follow the lane to Llanbedr out of Crickhowell. At the Llanbedr turn off (right) continue ahead. Where the road splits at a white cottage, continue ahead and cross the little stone bridge spanning the stream in Cwm Banw.*

Parking: *Parking space near the bridge. Grid Ref; SO 234 228. There is space for 4 or 5 cars immediately past the bridge.*

Please note: *No facilities en route.*

Going: *Easy.*

Terrain: *Mostly good paths and bridleways. The stretch passing through Park Wood can be muddy in areas. This walk is an absolute treat on a sunny autumn day, the remote wooded valley really showing off its beauty to full advantage.*

The Walk

1.   From the parking space, walk towards the bridge and turn right over a way-marked stile. Follow the sign uphill to leave the field over a stile. Join a stony track following signs 'to the mountain', and then ascend gently up the track to a junction of gates. Continue straight ahead passing through the gate.

2.   Trend to your right and continue ahead with a stone wall on your right. The path (in fact a bridleway) is not obvious here. At the end of the field, cross over a stile into a plantation (Park Wood) and follow the bridleway ahead, still keeping the stone wall on your immediate right. This section can be quite muddy.

Look over the wall for stunning views up the full length of the Grwyne Fechan valley.

3.   After a while the wall is replaced by a fence, and then by forestry. Continue straight ahead you eventually come to an area which has been heavily harvested. Where the bridleway joins up with a well defined forest track coming in from the right, with a

The fire beaters on your left

The right of way arrows on the trees

row of fire beaters on your left, cross the track to continue along the bridleway, following the right of way arrows.

4.   Follow the bridleway to leave the plantation by a wooden gate, erected by 'The King's Own Border' (a misprint of Borderers) as part of 'Exercise Dipper' on behalf of the National Park Authority.

5.   Continue ahead along the bridleway; the open lower slopes of Taltrwynau up to your left, and fields down to your right. Cross two stiles and follow the bridleway as it contours the slope. About 2 miles (3.2 kilometers) out of the forest a bridleways comes up from the right (Macnamara's Road). The spot where

Leave the forest through this gate

Grwyne Fechan

the bridleways join is almost directly opposite a small shed on the far side of the valley, at a junction of the fences, in the field below a large plantation (Twyn-du Forest).

Above Grwyne Fcehan valley

Macnamara's Road leads to the Hermitage, deep in the Grwyne Fechan Valley. It is said that the house was built to accommodate one of the philandering squire Macnamara's mistresses. Judging by the size of the ruins, the original house must have been of some considerable size. It was also built in a rather remote location and can't have been much for the aforementioned mistress if the weather was 'in' as the squire was out!

6.   Turn right and descend the 'road', crossing Afon Grwyne Fechan over a small stone bridge. (A little before you reach the bridge there is a delightful picnic spot, downstream for a small waterfall – just a thought). Having crossed the bridge, pass through a gate and ascend the bridleway to the right as it climbs gently across fields, passing through three gates to make its way back down the valley.

7.   At the point where it meets the gateway to Tal-y-Maes Farm, with a plantation on the left, the bridleway gives way to tarmac. Continue down the stony lane to the stone bridge, crossing the river, just before the Hermitage, on the left. Continue along the lane, passing through a gate, to meet a junction, just after Cwm Farm down on the left. From here, it is possible to return directly to the start by continuing ahead, but the more rewarding (if a little longer) option is to take the left fork,

Pass through this gate to continue along the bridleway

Grwyne Fechan and Macnamara Road

Old Chapel at Grwyne Fechan

signposted as being unsuitable for heavy vehicles, down to the river. The lane, narrow in places, runs alongside the river, passing 'The Old Chapel Grwyne Fechan'.

8.   Continue along the lane as it crosses the river again, at Pontyfelin, (the house on your left before the bridge used to be a mill) and stay with it as it swings to the right. At the next junction, keep ahead and cross the river at Bont Farm, where it is joined by the Cwm Banw River, actually under the bridge. Ascend the hill and, at the next junction by a cottage, turn right. Continue down this lane to the start of the walk.

Originally published in
Circular Walks in the Black Mountains

by Nick Jenkins

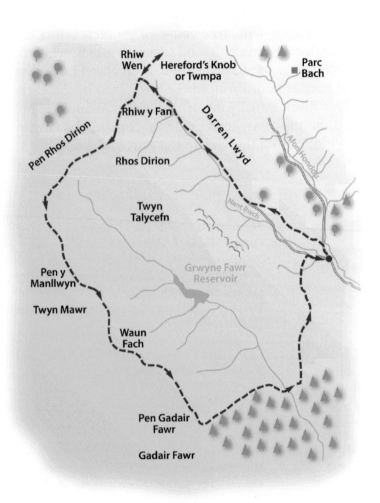

Walk 16
Capel-y-Ffin –
a hike up to the high spot

Walk details

Approx distance: *9 Miles/14.4 kilometres*

Approx time: *5 – 6 hours*

O.S. Maps: *Landranger Sheets 161 (Abergavenny & the Black Mountains) 1:50,000*
Outdoor Leisure Sheet 13 (Brecon Beacons National park – Eastern Area) 1:25,000

Start: *Capel-y-Ffin roadside, Grid Ref; SO 255 315*

Access: *The walk starts and ends at the small hamlet of Capel-y-Ffin, in the Vale of Ewyas (Dyffryn Euas). Take the narrow road that leads north up the valley from Llanfihangel Crucorney, through Llanthony (Llanddewi Nant Hondi), or south from Hay-on-Wye (Y Gelli Gandryll), over the Gospel Pass (Bwlchyrefengyl).*

Parking: *Capel-y-Ffin roadside. Do park considerately and don't block gates. Grid Ref; SO 255 315*

Please note: *No facilities en route.*

Going: *Strenuous.*

Terrain: *Mostly good paths and bridleways. Some lane walking. The section between Waun Fach and Penygadair Fawr is very glutinous after wet weather. Take care, too, on the rather steep descent from Penygadair Fawr down to the Grwyne Fawr valley, alongside Nantygadair Fawr (brook).*

Capel-y-Ffin

The Walk

1.   From the stream (Nant-Bwch) passing through the hamlet of Capel-y-Ffin, head north up the metalled road for about 300 yards (273 meters). Turn left over a stile and cross the field to the top right corner. Continue along the path as it passes between the buildings of Pen-y-Maes, and then pass through a gate. Keep on the path as it climbs the hillside. Join a bridleway coming in from your right and continue ahead. After a while the bridleway joins a metalled lane, leading to Blaen-bwch farm.

The hamlet of Capel-y-Ffin amply repays an exploratory stroll in its own right. The name is Welsh for 'chapel on the border', situated as it is just inside both the Gwent County and Wales boundary. There are, in fact, two chapels here, the well known whitewashed church near the roadside, and behind it, across Afon Honddu, a Baptist chapel, both of 18th

Capel-y-Ffin and Darren Lwyd

century origin. The wooden, louvered chimney of the church gives it a sort of squat, owl look. Inside the layout is very simple, with a pulpit dating from 1786, and a gallery, well worth exploring for the bird's eye view down into the building. Look out, too, for the immortal words engraved on the east window 'I shall lift up mine eyes unto the hills'.

View back down the valley towards Capel-y-Ffin

The Baptist chapel was built in 1737, and is tucked away under the hillside. From the upper corner of the graveyard there is a fine view of the chapel against the backdrop of the hill of Y Darren Lwyd, rising high over Capel-y-Ffin. Quite which chapel is referred to

Above Capel-y-Ffin in the Black Mountains

in the name of this solitary hamlet is not clear. There is, strictly speaking, one church and one chapel, so it may well be the Baptist Church, despite its comparative obscurity when compared to the better known church.

On the western side of the stream are the remains of the monastery of Llanthony Tertia, established by the Reverend Lester Lyne in 1870.

View down the Rhiangoll Valley

2.   Pass through two gates at the farm; the lane here returns to being a bridleway. Continue ahead along the bridleway, keeping Nant-bwch below you on your left, until you finally reach the northerly escarpment overlooking the Wye Valley (Dyffryn Gwy). From here turn right to follow the edge of the scarp and gradually ascend to the summit of Twmpa or, perhaps more poetically, Lord Hereford's Knob.

Twmpa, or Lord Hereford's Knob, at 2,263 feet (690 meters) offers a superb panoramic view north west across the Wye Valley (Dyffryn Gwy). The answer to the question why Lord Hereford's Knob (and which Lord Hereford?) has yet been uncovered.

3.   Retrace your steps to the point where the bridleway met the escarpment. Continue ahead along a path, the wide vista of the Wye Valley stretching away to your right. The path gently ascends to the summit of Rhosdirion, the top itself known as Pen-Rhosdirion.

4.   Continue ahead, dropping down slightly, to meet a track (officialy designated a 'Road used as a Public path') coming up on your left from the Grwyne Fawr Valley. Don't turn left down the track (unless a short-cut is the objective), but continue ahead for about 200 yards (182 meters), climbing the gently sloping ridge to the top of Penymanllwyn. Below on the right is the beautiful Rhiangoll Valley, across which can be clearly seen the great hump of Mynydd Troed.

5.   Continue up the incline, the gradient flattening out somewhat after Penymanllwyn has been crossed. From here, continue ahead across a very wet and boggy plateau (we are talking waders

*Trig point at the
summit of
Pen-Rhosdirion*

Rocks on the summit of Waun Fach

here after wet weather!) to the summit of Waun Fach. By way of consolation after the bog trot, you have now arrived at the highest point in the Black Mountains, at 2,660 feet (811 meters).

6. With Waun Fach behind you, continue along the broad ridge to the next, and frankly, rather more exciting, summit of Penygadair Fawr, marked by a large and conspicuous cairn. From here make your way down to the left corner of the now felled Mynydd Ddu Forest, ahead on your left.

7. At the corner of the forest turn left downhill, keeping the forest boundary fence on your right. Take care here; the path is quite steep in place, and can be muddy. On reaching the valley bottom, cross the stile on the right and follow the path to find an appropriate place to cross Afon Grwyne Fawr (using the stones in

Views from Chwarel y Fan ridge

Cairn on the summit of Penygadair Fawr

the river). After crossing the river, turn left on the track (which would lead you to the dam of the Grwyne Fawr reservoir) and walk back up to the gate.

8.   Start to ascend the lower slopes of Chwarel y Fan opposite, keeping the forest edge on your right. Cross a bridleway and continue ahead up the steep slope (no obvious path) but keeping close to the boundary of the forest on the right. Turn left onto a path as it emerges from the forest. Follow the path as it ascends the slope at a 45° degree angle to crest the ridge of Chwarel y Fan.

9.   The path drops to the left once over the ridge and picks its way easily through the rocks of Tarren yr Esgob. Continue ahead, passing the site of a monastery on your right, to join a metalled lane. Turn right along the lane and return to the start at Capel-y-Ffin.

Originally published in
Circular Walks in the Black Mountains

by Nick Jenkins

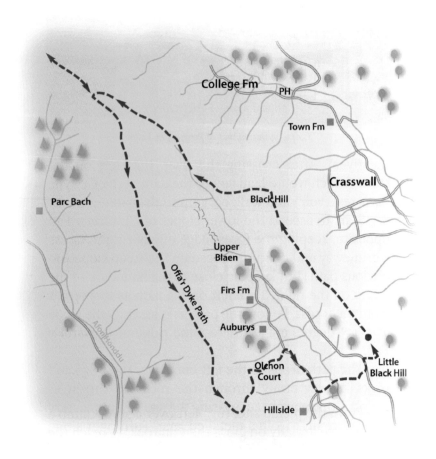

Walk 17
Hay Bluff – on the border

Walk details

Approx distance: *9 Miles/14.4 kilometres*

Approx time: *5 – 6 hours*

O.S. Maps: *Landranger Sheets 161 (Abergavenny & the Black Mountains) 1:50,000*
Outdoor Leisure Sheet 13 (Brecon Beacons National park – Eastern Area) 1:25,000

Start: *Black Hill picnic site, Grid Ref; SO 288 329*

Access: *The walk starts and ends near Llanfeuno, beneath the Cat's Back Ridge, a spur leading south of the Black Hill.*

Parking: *Picnic Site at Black Hill Grid Ref; SO 288 329*

Please note: *No facilities en route.*

Going: *Strenuous.*

Terrain: *Good clear paths, muddy in places after rain, and country lanes.*

The Walk

1. From the picnic site, turn left over a stile. Climb a steep path, initially on grass then on rock, to reach the fairly exposed ridge of Crib-y-garth. There is a choice here; either opt for the path which takes to the crest of the ridge, or a path just below the ridge may be selected. (The ridge is hardly the stuff of Crib Goch in Eryri (Snowdonia), but if you prefer not to perform acrobatics there is, at least, a Plan B.) Either way,

Hay Bluff

follow your chosen path as it makes its way north-west to the trig point on the Black Hill at 2,101 feet (640 meters), clearly visible ahead and slightly to the right.
2.   From the trig point take the wide path leading ½

Cat's Back Ridge

left. Stay with the path as it contours the hillside, rising ahead and to the right, which then gradually contours to the left. The head of the Vale of Olchon is now behind you, to the left about 1½ miles (2.4 kilometers) past the trig point on the Black Hill, the path meets the Offa's Dyke Path at right angles at the foot of a slope on the left.

View of Cat's Back Ridge leading to Black Hill

3. Carry straight on the path which makes an obvious bee-line for the trig point on the summit of Hay Bluff, about ½ mile (800 meters) ahead. From here, there is a terrific view across the wide stretch of the Wye Valley (Dyffryn Gwy) for as far as the eye can see.

Hay Bluff, at 2,220 feet (677 meters) is the high spot of this walk, and is sometimes referred to as Pen y Beacon. Although not quite as high as its southerly neighbour, the Black Hill, at 2,306 feet (703 meters) the views all around are stunning; north across the expanse of the Wye Valley (Dyffryn Gwy) with its patchwork fields, west across Twmpa and on to the central Beacons, south along the high ridge to the River Severn (Afon Hafren), and east across the agricultural lands of

Trig Point on the summit of Black Hill

The summit of Hay Bluff

Trig point on the summit of Hay Bluff

Herefordshire. On a hot summer day there is a perverse pleasure to be gained from sitting on the western edge, watching people toiling up the steep slope from the Gospel Pass (Bwlchyrefengyl), some 700 feet (214 meters) below.

4.   With your back to the trig point, retrace your steps along the path, heading south, to rejoin the Offa's Dyke Path. Make two short, sharp ascents to gain height of the broad top ahead. The top is not named on the OS maps but is locally known as Black Mountain (Grid Ref; SO 255 353). The path continues across Black Mountain in a south-easterly direction, with views of Waun Fach and Pen y Gadair Fawr to the west, and Crib-y-Garth (encountered earlier) to the east.

5.   As you descend gently from the summit of Black Mountain you will come across a large expanse of bare ground, covered with sun bleached pebbles and rocks that for the entire world look like a lunar landscape.

Cross the lunar landscape, your way marked by a series of cairns (28 at the last count).

6. Continue along the path until you reach a neat stone signpost at ground level, on your left, indicating Capel-y-Ffin to your right and Olchon Valley to your left. As a guide, the signpost is just about level with the road leading up to the picnic site on the other side of the valley, where you earlier started.

The sign post on your left which indicates Olchon Valley to the left and Capel-y-Ffin to the right

7. Turn left, downhill; the initially ill-defined path gradually improving into a more obvious track. The track zigzags down the hillside, offering beautiful views down almost the entire length of the Olchon Valley. At a fork in the path, take the left path, indicated by a way marker.

8. At the bottom continue ahead, through a gate, into a field. Keep to the right of the field to pass through a second gate into a lane. Turn right at the lane, to pass both Olchon Court and Beili-

At this way marker take the path going to the left.

bach Farm on your left. Cross a stile about 100 yards (91 meters) past Beli-bach, on the left, into a field.

9.   Keeping to the left of the field continue ahead, following the way markers. After about 200 yards (182 meters) the path descends to a footbridge crossing Nant Olchon (brook). Cross the footbridge and ascend, ½ right, up a track. Follow the track as it slowly fades to an obscure path, keeping to the right of the field, which is well way marked.

10.   The path continues to climb the hillside away from the brook and finally emerges at Black Hill Farm, part hidden in the trees. Cross to the stile opposite and continue along through the garden of the farm to a gate, in the top right corner. Continue along the path (straight ahead) alongside the brook to another stile.

Bear left after the stile following the way marker. Continue to climb the hill until you emerge on the lane. Turn left at the lane and, shortly afterwards turn right, up another lane, and back to the start.

Take this stile on your left into a field

Another view of Hay Bluff

Originally published in
Circular Walks in the Black Mountains

by Nick Jenkins

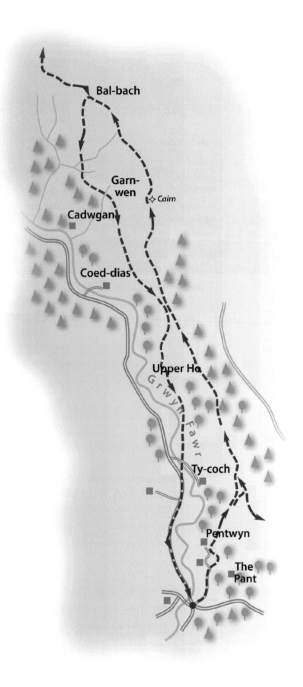

Walk 18
Cwm-iou – the ridge of revenge

Walk details

Approx distance: *9 Miles/14.4 kilometres*

Approx time: *5 – 6 hours*

O.S. Maps: *Landranger Sheets 161 (Abergavenny & the Black Mountains) 1:50,000*
Outdoor Leisure Sheet 13 (Brecon Beacons National park – Eastern Area) 1:25,000

Start: *Road junction at Pont Esgob, Grid Ref; SO 285 212*

Access: *The walk starts and ends near the road junction at Pont Esgob, on the minor road between Lower Cwm-yoy (Cwm-iou) (Stanton) and Forest Coal Pit.*

Parking: *Pull-in by a telephone box, enough room for 4 or 5 cars. Grid Ref; SO 285 212*

Please note: *No facilities en route.*

Going: *Strenuous because of its length.*

Terrain: *Country lanes, green lanes, farm track and good hill paths. Path can be muddy on the return (mainly alongside the wall running back to Dial Garreg).*

The Walk

1. From the car, walk back to the road junction, and turn left up the lane signposted as a No Through Road. Climb steadily up the hill, first passing on the right the driveway to 'The Pant' farm, and shortly after, 'New

The magnificent ridge above the Vale of Ewyas

Inn' farm on the left. Where the road splits take the right road. Ignore the concrete driveway on the right, but stay on the lane, which becomes a green lane.

2.	Follow the green lane as it contours the hillside. Keep an eye out for horses and riders along here – it is popular route for trekking (look carefully where you place your boots too!). At the gate, turn ½ right up a clear track onto open moorland. A stone wall appears on the left. Where the track and wall converge, continue ahead up the hillside to meet a broad grassy track at right angles.

3.	From here it is a fairly short and obvious stroll to the summit of 'Gaer', the Iron Age promontory fort on

Cairn on the summit of Gaer

the right. The extra effort is well rewarded in terms of both views and interest. The prominent hill to the right is the Sugar Loaf (*Mynydd Pen-y-Fâl*). Retrace your steps from the hill fort to the junction of paths and continue straight ahead.

Twyn-y-gaer, at 1,399 feet (426 meters) is an Iron Age encampment. It is oval in shape and divided into 3 sections, collectively covering about 4 ½ acres. The main entrance is approached by a sunken passage and is well protected by a double embankment. Interestingly it is the middle of a line of three such forts, the other two being Crug Hywel to the west; and Tre-wyn to the east, at the southern edge of Hatterall Hill.

4. If you don't visit the hill fort, turn left along the track, the views of both the Grwyne Fawr valley on the left and the Vale of Ewyas on the right being particularly good. Keep your eye out for the landslip below Hatterall Hill as well as Cwm-iou church beneath it on the right. In about ½ mile (800 meters) pass through a gate and where the path splits, a short while after, take the right hand path; the split is identified by a solitary pine tree in the corner of a field on the left. (You can go left, but the super views up the Vale of Ewyas are better enjoyed from the right hand path.)

It's so strange to imagine the Grwyne Valley without a road running along its length, but this was the case until not so long ago. The road was completed in 1912, and only then as a means of access to the Grwyne Fawr Reservoir 'Works', and the village of Blaen-y-cwm, which was built to house the 'navvy' workforce.

Inside Cwm-iou church

Prior to that there had been a track running part way up the valley bottom, which then climbed along the hillside below Bâl Mawr. The road was built under contract for the Abertillery and District Water Board, under whose direction the construction on the reservoir started in 1912 and continued until 1928. The final bill for the whole reservoir project, comprising the reservoir, the non-existent village of Blaen-y-cwm (at the top of the valley, and two miles below the reservoir), the road (also overlaid with a railway line) and a tunnel and pipes from the site to the Nantydraenog reservoir, just outside Crosskeys, came to just over one million pounds, a hefty sum indeed in 1928. At the height of construction, the village of Blaen-y-cwm was home to around 400 workers and their families. Today, little remains to point to the massive efforts to construct such a challenging piece of infrastructure.

Dial Garreg

5.   After about 200 yards (182 meters) the two paths join up again at the Dial Garreg, an upright stone about 3 feet high and surrounded by boulders to form a small plinth. The stone in fact marks the junction of paths coming up from Ewyas as well as descending to Grwyne Fawr.

Dial Garreg is Welsh for the *Revenge Stone*, and is said to mark the site of an older and larger memorial stone, placed there to identify the spot where Norman Marcher Lord, Richard de Clare, was attacked and killed by Morgan ap Owen, and his followers. Morgan was Welsh Lord of Caerleon and, in 1135, a concerted effort was made by the Welsh to drive the Norman oppressors out of Wales, at a time of turmoil following the death of Henry I. De Clare had been accompanied for part of his journey by Brain de L'isle (of Fitzcount, as he was also known) as far as the mouth of Afon Grwyne Fechan. Quite possibly de Clare felt there was less likelihood of being attacked on an exposed ridge

Cairn at the summit of Garn Wen

Bâl Bach (to the right) and Bâl Mawr in the distance

than in the secluded and sheltered valley; if so, it was an error of judgment that cost him his life.

6.   Continue along the ridge, following the track, and make for a huge cairn ahead, marking the summit of Garn Wen. The track gently climbs out of the rather sheltered stretch after Dial Garreg and onto more open moorland, before depositing you gently at the cairn and 'dugout' shelter. Pass the cairn, built with engineering precision, and continue ahead along the track to the top of Bâl Bach.

Cairn at the path junction below Bâl Mawr

7.   From here the path is obvious as it descends to a cairn (a good old 'pile of stones' this time). This cairn, like Dial Garreg previously, also marks a junction of paths. It also marks the start of

the stony path ascending Bâl Mawr, the summit of which at 1,990 feet (606 meters) supports both a trig point (OSBM S7281) and an excellent view of the continuation of the ridge as far as Chwarel y Fan, at 2,228 feet (679 meters). If you feel energetic, the continuation on to Chwarel y Fan is a fine extension to the walk. However, you should return to this point for the return leg.

Trig point at the summit of Bâl Mawr

8. Retrace your steps from the summit of Bâl Mawr down to the 'pile of stones' passed earlier. Turn right onto a path and, about 20 yards (18 meters) later, take the left fork. This will bring you safely down to a broad path contouring the hillside above Grwyne Fawr, just above the treeline, and running alongside a stone wall.

9. Turn left onto the path and follow it, firstly along the top of the forest edge, and then across open moorland. (The path can be very muddy along here, especially after rain).

Dial Garreg

Following the stone wall will bring lead you to this gate

The path will eventually lead you back to Dial Garreg. However, about 150 yards (136 meters) before the stone, and 200 yards (182 meters) before the stone wall just past it on the right, take a track leading ½ right. Follow the track as far as the stone wall. Keep on the track as it hugs the wall, now on your left, as far as a gateway.

10. Pass through the gateway into a green lane, fenced on both sides. The lane leads down to Upper House. Pass through the farmyard and, keeping the farmhouse

Tabernacle Chapel

on your right, leave it through a second gate (follow way markers through the farmyard). Descend a tarmac lane through a field to pass the house of Ty Mawr on your right. Continue down the lane to arrive at Tabernacle Chapel and the Grwyne Fawr river. The chapel graveyard is worth a short visit – there are some beautifully carved and inscribed headstones.

11. From the chapel, cross the river bridge and turn left down the road which runs the length of the Grwyne Valley, to return to the start.

Originally published in
Circular Walks in the Black Mountains

by Nick Jenkins

Splendid scenery in the Black Mountains

Best Walks in Wales

A series of guide books to take you to every corner of this magnificent walking country

- Short family walks
- Excellent coastal walks
- Hill and mountain walks & panoramic views
- Level lakeside and valley walks
- Woodland and nature walks
- Fascinating heritage and history guides
- Clear coloured maps
- Route photos and attractions on the way
- Updated directions

www.carreg-gwalch.com

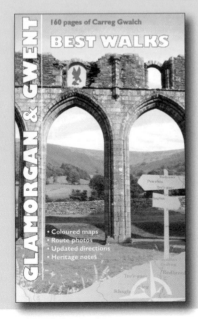

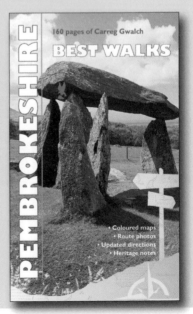

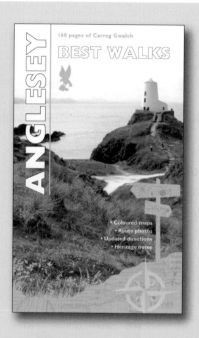

160 pages of Carreg Gwalch

BEST WALKS

ANGLESEY

- Coloured maps
- Route photos
- Updated directions
- Heritage notes

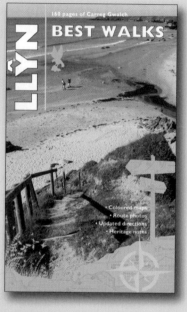

160 pages of Carreg Gwalch

BEST WALKS

LLŶN

- Coloured maps
- Route photos
- Updated directions
- Heritage notes

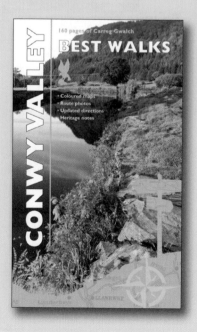

160 pages of Carreg Gwalch

BEST WALKS

CONWY VALLEY

- Coloured maps
- Route photos
- Updated directions
- Heritage notes

CENTRAL WALES

160 pages of Carreg Gwalch
BEST WALKS

• Coloured maps
• Route photos
• Updated directions
• Heritage notes

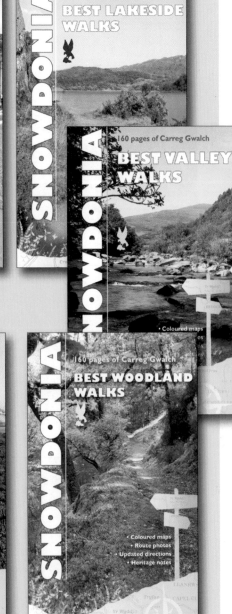

SNOWDONIA

160 pages of Carreg Gwalch
BEST LAKESIDE WALKS

NOWDONIA

160 pages of Carreg Gwalch
BEST VALLEY WALKS

• Coloured maps

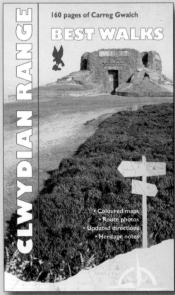

CLWYDIAN RANGE

160 pages of Carreg Gwalch
BEST WALKS

• Coloured maps
• Route photos
• Updated directions
• Heritage notes

SNOWDONIA

160 pages of Carreg Gwalch
BEST WOODLAND WALKS

• Coloured maps
• Route photos
• Updated directions
• Heritage notes